グローバル時代の英語

宮本陽一郎・大橋理枝・クリスティ コリンズ

JN060750

グローバル時代の英語（'22）

©2022　宮本陽一郎・大橋理枝・クリスティ コリンズ

装丁・ブックデザイン：畑中　猛

s-34

まえがき

　この授業では、ただ単に英語を学ぶというより、英語を学ぶということの意味について、みなさんと 15 回の授業を通じて考えていきたいと思っています。そして英語で書かれたテキストを読み、英語によるプレゼンテーションやスピーチを聞くことを通じて、この問題について考えてみましょう。英語と接しつつ深く考える経験によって初めて得られるような語学力を、この授業では目指したいと思っています。

　放送大学の授業の履修者のみなさんの中には、社会人としての経験をお持ちの方が、一般の大学よりはるかに多く含まれます。そういうみなさんは、みなさん自身の語学力のみならず、次の世代の日本人の語学力や、英語を学ぶ姿勢に、影響力と責任を持つ立場にいらっしゃいます。そういうみなさんが、英語を学ぶということの意味について考える機会を持つことは、たいへん重要な意味を持ちます。

　そして英語を学ぶことの意味は、21 世紀に入り確実に変化しました。

　現在では全世界で 10 億人を超える人が英語を用いてコミュニケーションを行っており、そのうち母語話者は 3 億 8 千人に満たないとされます。みなさんのような英語非母語話者のほうが、多数派になったわけです。英語は碧眼金髪の「ネイティヴ・スピーカー」の言葉ではなくなりました。

　かつて日本の大学の教室で英語の授業をするとき、履修している学生たちが将来において英語を実際に使う可能性は、想定するのがきわめて難しかったかもしれません。現在では、逆に日本人オンリーそして日本語オンリーの職場を想像することのほうが難しくなりました。社内公用語を日本語から英語に切り替えた日本企業も少なくありません。

　そのような時代にふさわしい英語の教え方とは何か——私たち教員は、ひとりひとりそれについて真剣に考えるわけですが、これは教員だけで答えの出せる問題ではありません。学習者であるみなさん、学習者の親や家族や上司でもあるみなさんと、ともに考えていくべき問題でしょう。

　そのためにこの授業ではグローバル時代の英語のあり方について論じた論説文のみならず、インターネット上の TED Talk のプレゼンテーション、そしてインタビューを教材とします。母語話者の英語と非母語話者の英語をともに扱っています。

　とりわけ日本に在住し、日本の社会をその一員として支えている外国人の方々にインタビューすることができたことを嬉しく思います。出身地は、スコットランド、カナダ、フィリピン、中国、イランと多様です。そのような多様な背景の人々が、日本に居を定め、英語を用いつつ日本社会を支えてくださっている――それがグローバル化していく日本の姿でしょう。インタビューの中では教科書の英語とは違うグローバル英語をじかに聞いていただくことができます。

　この印刷教材の使い方について簡単に説明します。

【Understanding the Contents】　この部分には、内容の読み取り／聞き取りのための、ごく簡単な設問を用意してあります。読む前／聞く前に設問と選択肢に目を通しておいてください。私たちが母語を読んだり聞いたりするとき、まったく白紙で読んだり聞いたりすることはありません。あらかじめ頭の中に枠組みができていて、その範囲の中で必要な追加情報をえたり、思い違いを修正したりします。この設問はそのような枠組みをあらかじめ頭の中に作る役割を果たします。英文和訳という作業になるべく頼らずに、必要な情報を読み取ったり聞き取ったりできるようになることが大切です。

【The Opinions】　各章の中から、ここだけはしっかり理解しておきたいという箇所を "Focus" として取り出して、放送授業の中で徹底的に解説します。巻末の解答欄には全訳も用意してあります。ここについてはみなさん各自で翻訳してみることも、よい練習になるでしょう。日本語に置き換えることそのものを目的とはせず、書き手／話し手の思考の展開をしっかりとつかめるまで読み込んでいきましょう。

【Today's Vocabulary】　このセクションでは、各章の中から、ぜひ身につけておきたい単語を5つ程度ピックアップして、他の用例とともに

挙げてあります。ヴォキャブラリー力は、知っている単語の数だけでは測れません。頻繁にしかもさまざまな意味合いで使われる重要単語をどこまでマスターするかが決定的に重要です。その意味で必要な重要単語の数は数百語に過ぎません。このセクションについては、ぜひ辞書を読んで学習してください。辞書に挙げられたさまざまな用法・用例を読み、印刷教材に挙げられたいくつかの用例を理解できるようにしましょう。しっかりと復習してください。

【Appendix】　インタビュー全文のテープ起こしです。言い淀みや言い直しなどもそのまま採録しています。放送授業でインタビューの音声を聞くときには、こちらを参照すれば、聞こえてくるほとんどすべての音が活字化されています。そのほうが安心感を持って聞けるという方は、活用してください。また時間的制約のために放送授業では残念ながら割愛した部分も再録してありますから、インタビューの内容に関心を持った方は、ぜひ自力で読んでみてください。

　英語の授業としてはやや異色の印刷教材そして放送授業となりましたが、不抜の忍耐力で印刷教材の作成を見守ってくださった編集者の香原ちさとさん、放送授業の製作について主任講師たちの気まぐれに臨機応変に対応してくださったディレクターの小林敬直さんと音声技術担当の小田嶋洋さん、シンガポール英語について現地でのインタビューにご協力いただいた前田瑞絵さんとオウ・チャイ・ランさん、印刷教材の匿名査読（フレンドリー・アドバイス）の労をとり本書の最初の読者となってくださった先生——たくさんのみなさんのお力を借りて、この授業は完成しました。この場を借りて心より御礼を申し上げたいと思います。

2021 年 10 月

宮本　陽一郎

大橋　理枝

クリスティ　コリンズ

6

目次

8

Part I

English as Lingua Franca

Chapters 1 ～ 3

(扉)

Chapter 1	Ma Shwe Sin Win (Cynthia), "Not good with names: Local name customs in a global village"

▲ミャンマー映画博物館まえのトロフィー像
（写真：ウィキペディアより）

Cynthia Ma Shwe Sin Win is currently the Executive Director/ Head of APAC FICC eSales at J.P. Morgan, Singapore. Cynthia is interested in how names are given and understood in different cultures. In her talk, Cynthia shares how and why her own name evolved as she moved from Myanmar, to Australia, and eventually to Singapore.

[1] <u>Many people know me as Cynthia Win, but the name given to me at birth was Ma Shwe Sin Win</u>. And I was born in Myanmar, this beautiful Southeast Asian country formerly known as Burma[1]. If you look at the four words that make up my name, can you guess which is my last name? Well, the answer is, I don't have a last name[2]. The first one Ma is an honorific which stands for Miss. Shwe Sin means "pure gold", which is also the name of our Academy Award trophy in Myanmar[3]. My mom must have been a huge fan of the movies. The last word Win means "shining",

1）1948 年にビルマ連邦としてイギリスから独立。1988 年に社会主義体制が崩壊し、ミャンマー連邦となった。ミャンマー連邦共和国となったのは 2011 年から。〈https://www.mofa.go.jp/mofaj/press/pr/wakaru/topics/vol93/〉
2）ウィキペディアの「アウンサンスーチー」のページには「この名前は、姓を有していません。姓に見える部分まで含めて、個人名の一部です。」と書かれている。〈https://ja.wikipedia.org/wiki/%E3%82%A2%E3%82%A6%E3%83%B3%E3%82%B5%E3%83%B3%E3%82%B9%E3%83%BC%E3%83%81%E3%83%BC〉名前に姓がないのはミャンマーに限らない。インドネシアの独立に際して主導的な役割を果たしたスカルノもこの名のみでフルネームである〈https://kotobank.jp/word/%E3%82%B9%E3%82%AB%E3%83%AB%E3%83%8E-83461〉。大橋が知っているインド出身の人も名前だけしかなく姓を持っていなかった。
3）ミャンマー映画界では芸術的および技術的に優れた作品を 1952 年から毎年表彰している（1963 年、1986 年、1987 年、1988 年を除く）。〈https://en.wikipedia.org/wiki/Myanmar_Motion_Picture_Academy_Awards〉トロフィーは頭上に両手で星を掲げる形。〈https://www.facebook.com/Myanmar-Academy-Awards-385835318248128/〉

so basically my name means "shining pure gold Academy Award". I like it that it sounds brilliant and precious. This is my brother. His name is Maung Ye Yint Aung, and this is me [4]. As you can see, there is not a common word in our names to imply that we are related. Mind you [5], we are biological siblings with the same mother and father.

[2] <u>Now, you might find it puzzling: how we trace our ancestry without a last name?</u> We are equally puzzled by how the rest of the world insist that we must have a last name to fill in every application form. Forms in Myanmar don't require last names. Instead, they ask for name in full and father's name in full, just like this visa application form from the Myanmar Embassy. Recently I've received a LinkedIn [6] request from a person called Win Aung. I don't know who that was so I just ignore the request. A week later my dad called me and asked, "You didn't friend me on Facebook; now you are ignoring me on LinkedIn as well?" Who would have thought after he split up [7] his name U Tin Aung Win to fit in the first and last name boxes and became Win Aung? Even I couldn't **recognize** my dad's name.

---

4) もとの TED Talk の動画では本人ともう1人男性が写っている写真が映写されている。

5) ここでは「一言付け加えておきますが」という意味。

6) 「ビジネスに特化した世界最大の SNS」。世界中に 6.45 億人の登録者を持つ。〈https://about.linkedin.com/ja-jp〉

7) 分割する

[3] <u>Having no last name doesn't mean we don't have a system in naming our children.</u> Following the ancient Burmese astrology most babies are named based on the day of the week he or she is born. Babies born on Monday will have names beginning with a set of letters from the Burmese alphabet and a tiger **represents** them. Tuesday-born babies will have names beginning with another set of letters and a lion **represents them.** There are eight days in a week, but not to worry, Wednesday is divided into morning and afternoon **represented** by elephants with and without tusks. The eight animal statues of the week can be found at corners surrounding most pagodas in Myanmar. Obama was born on a Friday which makes him a guinea pig. Friday-borns like him are believed to be creative, sympathetic, and talkative[8].

[4] <u>Now let me **share** with you how my name has evolved over the years.</u> At birth, the name given to me was Shwe Sin. In 1990 my family migrated to Singapore where most of my Chinese friends have three words in their names with the last two words being their first names. So when I was introduced to my new eight-year-old friends in Singapore, they naturally concluded, like

---

8）八曜日はミャンマーでは伝統的な考え方で、曜日ごとに守護動物だけでなく支配星や方位もある。生まれ曜日は基本的性格や運勢に影響を与えると考えられており、ミャンマー人はほぼ必ず自分の生まれ曜日を知っているという。ミャンマーでは生まれ曜日によって本人の性格や他人との相性を見ようとするが、これは日本で行われている血液型占いと同様のものであるとのこと。〈https://www.aarjapan.gr.jp/activity/blog/sp/2007/0424_240.html〉

them, my first name must be the last two words; Sin Win. As I wasn't able to speak English or Chinese initially, I didn't think that explaining to them the roots of my name or advising what they should be calling me were important at that time. So most people I've met in Singapore know me as Sin Win. In 2008 I went to Australia for graduate studies and decided to **adopt** a Western name chosen by my mom Cynthia as my first name and Win as my last name. Why Cynthia? Well, because when written in Burmese c-y-n, cyn, uses the letters [sa] of the Burmese alphabet which suits the Tuesday-born me. As for Win, I want an easy name to remember and who wouldn't want Win as their last name, right?

[5] <u>When someone calls me as Shwe Sin today, that person must also be Burmese but I've grown so disassociated with my own name that it now takes me a while to **register** that is actually me</u>. When someone calls me Sin Win, that person must be someone I know from school or work in Singapore. When I'm called Cynthia, that must be an MBA[9] classmate, a client, or a colleague. Cynthia Win is great for the business world but parts of me do miss the little Shwe Sin that was left behind in Myanmar. In many parts of Asia such as in Singapore, more and more babies are given Western names for convenience and we will see many Davids, Cynthias, and Lindas in future. But there might not be any

---

9) Master of Business Administration の略。「経済学修士」と訳される。欧米のビジネススクールの大学院修士課程で経営学を専攻し、修了すると取得できる。

Shwe Sins left in the world. If we don't learn the names from other cultures and make it convenient for everyone to use their cultural birth names, will we still see traditionally meaningful names like "the shining pure gold Academy Award" in the next generations?

ကျေးဇူးတင်ပါတယ် ။ Thank you.

I. Understanding the Contents

下線を施した各パラグラフのトピック・センテンスを注意深く読み，それ以外は速読して，問1〜5に入る内容を，それぞれ選択肢a〜dの中から選びましょう。

問1　Cynthia さんの姓は……
   a. Ma
   b. Sin Win
   c. Ma Shwe Sin Win
   d. a〜c のいずれでもない

問2　第2パラグラフにある "Win Aung" という人物の正体は……
   a. ミャンマー大使館の関係者
   b. まったく面識のない人物
   c. Cynthia さんの父親
   d. Cynthia さんの兄

問3　ミャンマーにおいて人の名前は……

  a. 父方の家系をあらわす

  b. 母方の家系をあらわす

  c. 出身地をあらわす

  d. 生まれた曜日をあらわす

問4　Cynthia さんが "Cynthia" という名前を主に使うようになったのは……

  a. シンガポールに移住してから

  b. オーストラリアに留学してから

  c. アメリカに留学してから

  d. ビジネスを始めてから

問5　第1パラグラフと第5パラグラフに出てくる "the shining pure gold Academy Award" とは……

  a. 現代のグローバル化した世界を比喩的にあらわした表現である。

  b. 日本でいう「キラキラネーム」のことである。

  c. 現代のミャンマーの文化の多様性を指す表現である。

  d. Cynthia さんの名前の英語訳である。

II. The Opinions

プレゼンテーションの中の次の2つの部分を精読し，著者の主張をそれぞれ100字程度にまとめましょう。

Focus 1

Now, you might find it puzzling: how we trace our ancestry without a last name? We are equally puzzled by how the rest of the world insist that we must have a last name to fill in every application form. Forms in Myanmar don't require last names. Instead, they ask for name in full and father's name in full, just like this visa application form from the Myanmar Embassy.

Focus 2

Cynthia Win is great for the business world but parts of me do miss the little Shwe Sin that was left behind in Myanmar. In many parts of Asia such as in Singapore, more and more babies are given Western names for convenience and we will see many Davids, Cynthias, and Lindas in future. But there might not be any Shwe Sins left in the world. If we don't learn the names from other cultures and make it convenient for everyone to use their cultural birth names, will we still see traditionally meaningful names like "the shining pure gold Academy Award" in the next generations?

III. Today's Vocabulary
以下の５つの単語について辞書を読み，さまざまな用例を理解した上で，
本文中での用例を日本語に訳してみましょう。

recognize
・He didn't recognize me at the party.
・She recognized that it was her fault.
・His talent was recognized by the people who saw the presentation.
Even I couldn't <u>recognize</u> my dad's name.

represent
・The sign "+" represents addition.
・She represented the entire university at the contest.
・The melody represents their love for each other.
・The depth of her feelings was difficult to represent in words.
・Her article represented him as a kind gentleman.
・She represents an ideal lady.
Babies born on Monday will have names beginning with a set of
letters from the Burmese alphabet and a tiger <u>represents</u> them.
Wednesday is divided into morning and afternoon <u>represented</u> by
elephants with and without tusks.

share
・We shared the profits among ourselves.
・We used to share one hotel room between four students when
  attending a conference.

· She shared her secrets with me.

· They share the housework and child-rearing responsibilities equally.

Let me <u>share</u> with you how my name has evolved over the years.

adopt

· They adopted the latest technology to cure the disease.

· It was historically not uncommon to adopt a son in Japan.

· She adopted a Western name as her nickname.

· The English word "i.e." is adopted from Latin.

In 2008 I went to Australia for graduate studies and decided to <u>adopt</u>
a Western name.

register

· You must register with the city office when you move in.

· All students must be registered before the semester starts.

· The thermometer registered the coldest temperature of the season
  this morning.

· His body movements registered irritation.

· The expression she made at that moment registered deeply in my
  memory.

I've grown so disassociated with my own name that it now takes me
a while to <u>register</u> that is actually me.

発展的課題

A. Cynthiaさんの場合と比較しながら，日本における姓名の使用方法の特異性について考えてみましょう。

B. 英語を用いるとき，あなたは自分自身の名前をどのように表記あるいは発音しますか？たとえば「新島 襄」という人物については"Niijima" "Jo" "Joe" "Joe Niijima" "Niijima Jo"のような選択肢があります。またそれを選択した理由を説明してください。

C. 以下のような本文中の表現を利用しながら，あなた自身の名前の由来を英語で説明してください。

Shwe Sin means "pure gold", which is also the name of our Academy Award trophy in Myanmar. [1]

The last word Win means "shining", so basically my name means "shining pure gold Academy Award". [1]

So most people I've met in Singapore know me as Sin Win. [4]

Case in point . . . [1]

It brings to mind . . . [2]

Let me tell you a story about . . . [5]

【コラム】　　■ ■　**How to Address People**　■ ■

Knowing how to properly address people can be a difficult and stressful thing for many of us. Different countries and cultures have different customs for addressing people according to age, gender, marital status, professional position, and so on. As such, it can be a bit tricky figuring out the best way to address people in another language, especially when you may be meeting for the first time.

In English, gender plays a role in the way people address each other with their family names. For example, for a man, regardless of age or marital status, he will be addressed as "Mister X". On the other hand, for women, young(er) women are usually addressed as "Miss X", and then become "Missus X" (Mrs. X) when they marry (regardless of age). Once women reach middle age, they may be addressed as "Missus X" or "ma'am" (short for madam) to indicate that they are no longer considered to be *young* women—an issue which many women find rather sexist and ageist. In the 1960s, American feminist Sheila Michaels campaigned to adopt the use of "Ms." so that women did not have to be defined by their marital status, and this has become very common in English-speaking countries. After all, the generic "Mr." works for men, so its feminine counterpart "Ms." makes good sense.

In Japan, the name order can be rather confusing since Japanese and non-Japanese names are given in reverse order. For example, while in Japan a person would list their family name first, and their given name second (i.e. Miyamoto Yoichiro), in Canada, a person would list their given name first, and their family name second (i.e. Kristie Collins). Due to this difference, many foreign people living in Japan find themselves being called by their first name rather than their family name by Japanese colleagues and acquaintances, as in "Kristie-san, nice to meet you!" In my case, I have always welcomed people calling me by my given name, so I am happy to have people address me as "Kristie-san" or "Kristie-sensei", but some non-Japanese people may prefer to be addressed by their family name. Likewise, many of my Japanese colleagues and acquaintances have asked me to call them by their given name, rather than their family name.

Since there may be some issues related to power and equality in the way we address each other, for instance with the use of "sensei" or "san" in Japan, it is probably best to ask someone how they prefer to be addressed. Using each other's preferred pronouns, titles, and names is a great way to forge respectful relationships and friendships.

(Kristie Collins)

Chapter 2
David Crystal, "The more things change . . ."

（写真提供：ユニフォトプレス）

David Crystal served more than ten years as a Chair in the Department of English Language and Applied Linguistics at the University of Reading, and is now Honorary Professor of Linguistics at the University of Wales, Bangor. Over his lifetime, Professor Crystal has worked as an editor, broadcaster, writer, and lecturer, and has published over 100 books, chiefly in the fields of English language studies, stylistics, and in the application of linguistics to clinical, religious, and educational contexts.

[1] <u>The notion of world English seems to have been around</u> [1] <u>for ever, but is actually very recent.</u> In the 1970s people were still coming to terms with [2] the idea that English was becoming global. It wasn't conceivable a generation before, according to Reg Close, thinking back to 1937: 'who could have imagined that English would **survive** as a *lingua franca* [3] ?' Randolph Quirk draws attention to the way the trend became apparent only after World War Ⅱ. And nobody had published books recognising [4] English as a global language when they were writing.

[2] <u>Our present-day concerns are **anticipated**.</u> Alfred ('Gim') Gimson was worried by deteriorating intelligibility in second-language communities, while a later contributor [5] emphasised [6] the need to retain local accents for identity. The tension between maintaining intelligibility and maintaining identity is still with us, as occasional difficulties of comprehension at any international conference illustrate. For Ron White, the solution was to recommend more than one model. And the possible complementarity of local and global perspectives later became a major theme, as seen in Shih-Chieh Chien.

1）存在して、出回って
2）（～に）慣れる
3）共通語、世界語（母語が異なる人々の間で意思伝達のために使われる言語）
4）この文章は基本的にイギリス英語で書かれているので、"recognising" と綴られている。アメリカ英語では "recognizing" と綴られる。
5）この Crystal の記事は The International Association of Teachers of English as a Foreign Language (IATEFL) の機関紙の 50 周年記念号の中の言語特集に寄せられたものなので、その特集に記事が載っている著者を指している。
6）アメリカ式の綴りでは "emphasized"。

[3] <u>In the 1970s, when the rise of new global Englishes was still in its infancy, there was uncertainty about their future.</u> Many felt they would have a short life, or **remain** only as 'low'[7] colloquial speech. Quirk predicted more would emerge, and he was right, his point being echoed twenty years later by David Graddol. What nobody predicted was how quickly these '<u>new Englishes</u>' would appear in an institutionalised [8] form, with written and spoken norms, local dictionaries and grammars, and an unselfconscious use in local literature. We have seen this happen in several countries. Today there is a much greater recognition of variety differences, and a level of mutual respect, than existed two generations ago.

[4] <u>For several contributors, this diversity is a real plus.</u> For Quirk, the strength of English lies in its geographical spread: if its use diminishes in one place, it is secure in another. By 1977 the global spread had, he felt, 'enough momentum . . . to carry it through[9] this century and the next without serious rival'. He was right about that too. He also predicted a lessening of use in some countries, as indigenous languages achieved greater presence, and with some

---

7）言語変種（language variety）を high/low と捉える発想に基づく。いわゆる「正統的」なものが high variety とされ、方言や混成言語などは low variety とされる。この場合は伝統的に英語母語話者とされている人たち（イギリス人、アメリカ人、オーストラリア人など）が話す英語が high variety であるのに対し、global English を low variety であると捉える見方を指す。

8）アメリカ式の綴りでは "institutionalized"。

9）〈人に〉（病気・難局などを）切り抜けさせる

resisting English; and this was later supported by Graddol, predicting an eventual fall in the proportion of English learners.

[5] <u>The contributors are **positive** about increasing diversity</u>. Graddol makes the important point that diversity is nothing new: 'we have already learned to live with a pluricentered[10] language', and **anticipates** greater tolerance of variety. Everyone now accepts the need for some kind of international standard, but we now realise[11] that this won't be a monolithic[12] thing. It will include variation, just as English has always done.

[6] <u>By the 1990s the question of how to handle variation in teaching was beginning to be debated</u>, and the contributors to the 1993 panel display the range of views we still discuss today. That decade brought increased recognition of the new complexity: life was no longer a simple question of British vs American English; other varieties were becoming influential, and the Internet began to expose learners to them in unprecedented ways. A common question was which variety would eventually dominate—presumably American English. What we now know is that, yes, American influence on other varieties has been great, but not so much that these other varieties have lost their identity. British English is still British, although showing more American features than a generation ago.

---

10) 中心が複数であること。
11) アメリカ式の綴りでは "realize"。
12) 異論を言う人のいない、一枚岩的な

[7] It is this scenario that fuelled [13] the alternative view that none of the traditional varieties would become dominant, but that some sort of new international English would **evolve**. For Close, this would be a 'common core', not a native-speaking variety. Graddol **anticipated** the development of an English 'not modelled on any one national variety'. There was a growing realization that research was needed. One contributor asks for a corpus [14] of international data—something we now see, for example, in the International Corpus of English and the Vienna Voice corpus. But the question of best practice **remains**. Another contributor asserts that until international English has been properly studied, we should stay with native-speaking norms. Chien emphasises [15] the need to make these norms communicatively **relevant**.

[8] Close asked: 'who could be bold enough to prophesy how much English and what kind of English will be used in the year 2017?' We are now almost there, and many of his concerns are still with us. His comment on the role of the teacher is as **relevant** today as it was then: 'the solid work of preserving English as a medium of international communication will fall upon classroom teachers, whose success will result largely from their steering a steady and consistent course'. The French have a phrase for it: 'plus ça change, plus c'est la même chose'.

---

13) アメリカ式の綴りでは "fueled"。
14) コーパス。言語学的分析のために収集された一群のデータ。
15) アメリカ式の綴りでは "emphasizes"。

I. Understanding the Contents

下線を施した各パラグラフのトピック・センテンスを注意深く読み，そ
れ以外は速読して，問1〜5に入る内容を，それぞれ選択肢a〜dの
中から選びましょう。

問1　グローバル英語という概念が生まれたのは……
　a. 産業革命期
　b. 大英帝国時代
　c. 第二次世界大戦直後
　d. 比較的最近

問2　第2パラグラフで述べられている懸念（ "Our present-day
concern"）とは……
　a. 国によって英語力の格差が生じてしまうこと
　b. 英語により他の言語が淘汰されてしまうこと
　c. 現実的には国際公用語としては機能しないこと
　d. ローカルな訛りを尊重するか、訛りのない標準的な英語を目指すか
　　というジレンマ

問3　第4パラグラフで述べられている "diversity" とは……
　a. 人種的な多様性
　b. 国ごとの言語の多様性
　c. 経済的格差
　d. 地域ごとの英語の多様性

問4　第7パラグラフで述べられている "the alternative view" とは……

 a. イギリス英語・アメリカ英語ではない，新しいタイプの英語が公
  用語になるという考え方

 b. 地域ごとに生じる英語の訛りを尊重した英語教育をしようという考え方

 c. 訛りのない英語を教えるための新しい教育法をあみだそうという
  考え方

 d. 英語以外の国際共通語を作ろうという考え方

問5　最終行にある 'plus ça change, plus c'est la même chose' という
フランス語の意味を文脈から推測しなさい。

 a. 変化が起きれば，必ず失われるものがある

 b. 変化が起きれば，数が増える

 c. 変化が起きるほどに，あらたに可能性が広がる

 d. 変化が起きるほどに，不変のものが明らかになる

II. The Opinions

プレゼンテーションの中の次の2つの部分を精読し，著者の主張をそれ
ぞれ100字程度にまとめましょう。

Focus 1

By the 1990s the question of how to handle variation in teaching
was beginning to be debated, and the contributors to the 1993 panel
display the range of views we still discuss today. That decade brought
increased recognition of the new complexity: life was no longer a
simple question of British vs American English; other varieties were

becoming influential, and the Internet began to expose learners to them in unprecedented ways. A common question was which variety would eventually dominate—presumably American English. What we now know is that, yes, American influence on other varieties has been great, but not so much that these other varieties have lost their identity. British English is still British, although showing more American features than a generation ago.

Focus 2

It is this scenario that fuelled the alternative view that none of the traditional varieties would become dominant, but that some sort of new international English would evolve. For Close, this would be a 'common core', not a native-speaking variety. Graddol anticipated the development of an English 'not modelled on any one national variety'. There was a growing realization that research was needed. One contributor asks for a corpus of international data—something we now see, for example, in the International Corpus of English and the Vienna Voice corpus. But the question of best practice remains. Another contributor asserts that until international English has been properly studied, we should stay with native-speaking norms. Chien emphasises the need to make these norms communicatively relevant.

III. Today's Vocabulary

以下の6つの単語について辞書を読み，さまざまな用例を理解した上で，本文中での用例を日本語に訳してみましょう。

survive

· The ship sank, but she survived.

· He was forced to survive through the winter without heat.

· The town may not be able to survive the recession.

· He is survived by his wife and two daughters.

It wasn't conceivable a generation before, according to Reg Close, thinking back to 1937: 'who could have imagined that English would survive as a *lingua franca*?'

anticipate

· The consequences cannot be anticipated.

· The test question was just what I anticipated.

· This fashion trend was anticipated from decades ago.

Our present-day concerns are anticipated.

Graddol makes the important point that diversity is nothing new: 'we have already learned to live with a pluricentered language', and anticipates greater tolerance of variety.

Graddol anticipated the development of an English 'not modelled on any one national variety'.

remain

· She remained in the top position.

· He had to remain in bed until the fever was gone.

· Is your enthusiasm still remaining?

· The task still remains to be done.

Many felt they would have a short life, or remain only as 'low' colloquial speech.

The question of best practice <u>remains</u>.

positive

- He decided to adopt a positive outlook regarding the issue.
- Don't just listen to the positive comments. Make sure you listen to the negative ones, too.
- She decided to take some positive actions to take care of the situation.
- "Are you sure?" "Yes! I'm absolutely positive."
- He tested positive for the disease.
- You get a positive number by multiplying two negative numbers.

The contributors are <u>positive</u> about increasing diversity.

evolve

- Fish evolved into amphibians.
- His company evolved into one of the largest enterprises in the country.

Some sort of new international English would <u>evolve</u>.

relevant

- Art may not seem relevant to people's lives, but in fact it is vital.
- He made sure that all the relevant documents were at hand.

Chien emphasises the need to make these norms communicatively <u>relevant</u>.

His comment on the role of the teacher is as <u>relevant</u> today as it was then.

発展的課題

A. "lingua franca"（国際的な公用語）は，なぜとりわけ第二次世界大戦後にその必要が認識されるようになったのでしょうか?

B. 現在の日本社会の中で，"lingua franca"はどのようなかたちで必要とされていますか?

C. 日本人特有の英語の発音（訛り）は，日本の英語教育の中で，どのようなかたちで許容するべき，あるいは許容すべきでないか，あなた自身の考えを述べてください。

【コラム】　　■ ■　パラグラフとは何か?　■ ■

　パラグラフは段落ではありません。パラグラフには明確な構造があります。

　みなさんが英語のセンテンスを読むときには、それに先立って主語と動詞という構造が頭の中にすでにあります。最初からひとつひとつの単語の意味を考える前に、このセンテンスの主語は何か、動詞は何かを考えます。主語が原則としてどこに出てくるかもわかっています。

　同様にパラグラフにも構造があります。主語にあたるもの、つまりそのパラグラフの論点は、原則的には第1センテンスにおかれます。これをトピックセンテンスと呼びます。それに続くいくつかのセンテンスは、トピックセンテンスに提示された論点をサポートする役割を担います。

　そのいちばんわかりやすい形は、3つ具体例を挙げるというやりかたです。英語では「なんでそんなことが言えるんだい?」というかわりに "Name three examples." ということがあります。つまり3つ具体例が挙げられれば、一応相手の主張に納得するということです。3つ具体例を挙げるというのが、説得の基本形と言ってもいいでしょう。

　パラグラフとは何か?　私なりに思い切りわかりやすく説明するとすれば、次の2つの方程式になります。

● 1=1

　つまり、〈1つのパラグラフは、かならず1つの論点で構成し、決して2つ以上のことを1つのパラグラフの中で言ってはいけない〉ということです。

● 1=1+3

　つまり〈1つのパラグラフは、1つのトピックセンテンスと、それをサポートする3つの具体例(など)で構成される〉というルールです。もちろん具体例を挙げるだけが説得方法ではありません。たとえば何がどうしてどうなったというプロセスや、因果関係を説明して、読者や聞き手を説得することもできます。あるいはトピックセンテンス

から演繹的に言えることを3つ程度挙げるということも、トピックセンテンスの意味する
ところをより明確にするために有効です。

　この2つの方程式は、英語が母語でない私たちにとってはグッドニュースです。つ
まりトピックセンテンスの意味をしっかりつかんでいれば、そのあとの3つのポイントのう
ち1つがわからなくても、2つわからなくても、場合によっては1つもわからなくても、書
き手の主張そのものを見失うことがありません。論理の流れそのものを見失うことが
ありません。逆に言うと、パラグラフの最後のセンテンスまでしっかり読まないと意味
を取り違ってしまうようなパラグラフは書くな、という文章作法です。

　パラグラフという概念は、歴史的にいくらでもさかのぼることができますが、それが
アメリカで作文教育の中核にすえられたのは、それほど古い出来事ではありません。
スプートニク・ショック直後の1958年に始まる国を挙げた教育改革の中で、小学校
の作文教育のカリキュラムにパラグラフ・ライティングの概念が導入されます。同じ時
期に大学ではアカデミック・ライティングを徹底的に訓練する「フレッシュマン・ライティ
ング・セミナー」が必修化します。

　英語が学術論文の実質的な公用語であるという現状のひとつの始まりをそこに見
出すことができるでしょう。

（宮本陽一郎）

Chapter 3

Conversation with Navid Sepehri

H. Sepehri-Amin is a principal researcher at the National Institute for Materials Science (NIMS), Japan. He was born in 1983 in Tehran, Iran, and moved to Japan in 2008 for his graduate studies. He received his PhD degree from the Graduate School of Pure and Applied Sciences from the University of Tsukuba in 2011. After three years as an ICYS (International Center for Young Scientists) fellow at NIMS (2011-2014), he has continued his research career as a permanent research staff member at NIMS since 2014.

K: Thank you so much for coming to talk with us today Navid. Would you be able to give us a little information about yourself and what you do?

N: Thank you very much for having me here. And I'm very happy that I can be part of your project. So my name is Navid. My family name is Sepehri-Amin. I'm from Iran and, well, I came to Japan in 2008 March—end of March—and since then I've been here. I never lived in any English-speaking country, and coming to Japan was my . . . maybe first country that I started living out of Iran.

K: Wow.

N: And I've been . . . practically living with my family all the time before coming to Japan. So it was kind of the first experience that I live by myself and in a foreign country.

K: Wow, that's really cool. Now when you first came to Japan were you expecting to stay here for a long time?

N: No. There is a movie of me saying goodbye to my parents and I just told them "Okay. See you soon." and "I will be back home in three years." So . . . it never happened.

K: Okay. So that would have brought us to 2011. OK. So what made you stay?

N: Well, actually, first was job. So my research and my goal for future research and career. So I started my PhD here and I never expected that I will just stay in Japan . . . even during my PhD I was looking about different choices, different opportunities. And . . . well . . . , life continued and, like, I got my PhD degree, I saw that I am still successful in the place that I was doing my research and all facilities enabled me to do whatever I wanted to do. And . . . like . . . more important than that, I met my current wife . . . my wife, in 2008 I met her, and we were always together. Although she was always fine to move anywhere with me, but we ended up continuing living here together.

K: That's wonderful.

N: Thank you.

K: And so what do you study, or what were you studying? And what do you do now?

N: So, my research. My major is material science[1].

K: Okay.

N: So I'm a material scientist and my PhD is on magnetic materials. It is more like material science and applied science and combination of that with physics and very old metallurgy[2] sometimes is included.

K: Yes, and so you are employed here in Tsukuba.

N: Yeah, so after my PhD I was post-doc[3] for a couple of years and I joined a research program called International Centre

1）材料科学。主として個体材料に関し、あらゆる基礎的な問題の連係的な理論的研究、およびその成果の工業的応用・開発までを含む広範な内容を持つ学問分野。〔ブリタニカ〕

2）冶金学。金属の製錬と精製、加工、合金製造などの技術系統と、金属組織学、物理金属学などの理論分野とを含む広い学術領域。多くの点で金属工学と一致するが、概念上は技術系統にやや重点がある。〔ブリタニカ〕

3）ポスドク。博士号を取得した研究者で、大学の専任教員職に就いていないことが多い。

for Young Scientists[4] and it's kind of tenure track position[5],
and after that I got permanent position in NIMS[6] and now I'm
principal researcher in National Institute for Materials Science.

K: Fantastic. And so that's a governmental agency?

N: That's right.

K: Yeah. Very cool. Okay. What languages can you speak and
where and when do you use them?

N: So, my mother's tongue is Farsi[7], so I kind of speak Farsi
and I can speak a little bit of English and also very little of
Japanese. And very little of Arabic.

K: You are very modest. And here in Japan, where do you have
a chance to use those different languages?

N: Well, English is my language at work. And also I still communicate
with my wife in English. We started communicating with
each other in English and it continues forever.

K: Right.

N: Although sometimes I change it to . . . like, my wife also can

---

4）「世界の優秀な若いポスドク研究者に独立した研究予算と自由な研究環境を提供することで、イノベーションとなるような研究を生み出す自立した若手研究者を育成するシステムの確立を目指し」て国立研究開発法人物質・材料研究機構の中に科学技術振興調整費の支援のもとで 2003 年から設立されたプログラム。
〈https://www.nims.go.jp/hr-development/icys/index.html〉
5）一定の審査期間を経て終身在職権（tenure）を取得することの内定した専任教員職。
6）国立研究開発法人　物質・材料研究機構。National Institute for Materials Science の略称。〈https://www.nims.go.jp/〉
7）現代ペルシャ語：イランおよびアフガニスタン西部で用いられ、アラビア文字で書かれる。〔ランダムハウス英和大辞典〕

speak Farsi and she is Japanese, Japanese is her mother tongue. And sometimes we speak to each other in Japanese, but that is not so often.

K: Okay.

N: So . . . but since my daughter was born in, like, 4 years and a half ago, she . . . well, I was very concerned about language for her and I studied a bit about it and I like to speak to her in Farsi, but when my wife is around she doesn't change between Farsi and Japanese. She listen to me in Farsi, most of the time she answer me in Japanese.

K: Okay.

N: So that's why I'm learning a lot of Japanese from her as well— new words and new words.

K: That's great. I do need to borrow her more[8]. And so at work, is everything in English? Or do you have to use any Japanese?

N: That's right. Everything is not in English, but some of my . . . like, I have foreigner students and postdocs. So with them I always use English and recently that . . . like . . . I'm more involved in some project, national projects or some collaboration with Japanese industries, I need to also use my Japanese capability.

K: Right, right.

8）インタビューしている Kristie とインタビュー相手である Navid はかなり親しく、家族ぐるみの付き合いがあるため、Kristie が Navid のお嬢さんともっと頻繁にお会いしたい、という趣旨のことをこのように表現したもの（そうすれば Kristie 自身がもっと日本語を教われるから、という含みがある）。

N: So, sometimes I communicate with people in Japanese, it's becoming faster than communicating with them in English.

K: Yeah.

N: And also I attend lots of domestic conferences and workshops that the main language is Japanese.

K: Right.

N: So I need to use Japanese as well.

K: Yeah, I think it's interesting that your first language is Farsi, and your wife Keiko's first language is Japanese and that you speak to each other in English.

N: That's right, that's right.

K: I think that's really cool. And so at home Niki, your daughter, is actually getting access to three languages.

N: That's right.

Sometimes we are like . . . talking with Keiko like . . . very simple example, like where can we go for dinner? And we just say that in English. And Niki answer where she wants to go for dinner and like, "Okay, how do you know what we said?" and "I know what you're talking about." And she's catching.

K: So fortunate.

N: She's actually smart.

K: That's great. I think it's also interesting that Keiko decided that she wanted to learn Farsi.

N: That's right.

K: So what motivated that for her?

N: Well, I think . . . well, my father kind of speak English, my mother to some extent, not much, and she wanted to communicate more with them.

K: Right.

N: Particularly my mother. And apart from that, her major is more related to . . . her major is social science, but her bachelor's degree was more related to language.

K: Okay.

N: And she has interest, so she studied, and I was very happy even though I was not with her at that time. She was in Iran by herself with my family,

K: Which is awesome.

N: and . . . like, I really enjoyed that when I saw her "Oh, she speaks lots of Farsi," and I'm very happy.

K: And I'm sure that . . . that effort on her part really, really must have meant a lot to your family.

N: That's right.

K: Yeah, that's so cool. And now how about for you speaking with her family? What language do you use?

N: Yeah, I speak Japanese with them, and in the beginning it was like . . . it's too complex, my case.

K: I think it's fantastic!

I. Understanding the Contents

インタビューを速読して，問1～5に入る内容を，それぞれ選択肢 a ～ d の中から選びましょう。

問1 ナヴィッドさんが日本に来たのは……
　a. 昨年初めて
　b. 2008 年
　c. 2011 年
　d. 幼少の頃

問2 ナヴィッドさんが日本に滞在することを決めた最大の理由は……
　a. 日本人と結婚したため
　b. 日本企業に就職したため
　c. 日本で研究するため
　d. 経済的理由のため

問3 ナヴィッドさんの専門分野は……
　a. 航空科学
　b. 文化人類学
　c. 物質科学／材料科学
　d. 日本史

問4 ナヴィッドさんの日本での最初の勤務先は……
　a. 一般企業
　b. 大学・研究機関
　c. 中学・高校
　d. 語学学校

問5 ナヴィッドさんが家庭内の会話で用いる言語は……
　a. 日本語のみ

b. 日本語とファルシ語

c. 日本語と英語とファルシ語

d. 英語のみ

II. The Opinions

インタビューの中の次の3つの部分を精読し、Navid さんの主張をそれぞれ100字程度にまとめましょう。

Focus 1

K: What do you see as the future of language communication in the world of science?

N: I don't think there will be a big change.

K: Okay.

N: So I think English will **remain** as the common language for communication in science field and worldwide. Well, however, there is a possibility with the current growth of economy in some countries and considering the population of for example, China or so, those like some **particular** languages like Chinese can play some major role in the future as well. But in terms of common language in science community, I think English will be the one.

K: Yeah, I suppose especially with the Internet and just this having . . . having this . . . in the cloud, research library of all of the writing in English, it's probably hard to **reverse** that now.

Focus 2

N: As you realize from this interview, if you listen my conversation, not reading the text, you see that I am not that fluent in English. So I was never shy to speak English. I know that I have lots of mistakes. I have lots of grammatical mistakes, I have lots of mispronunciation of the words that I'm saying. But Kristie as native speaker can completely understand me, what I'm saying.

K: A hundred percent.

N: So I'm not **embarrassed** of mispronouncing any word and remember that if you are speaking English as your second or third language, you need to remember that you are more powerful than a person who speaks one language even though if that is English as mother's tongue. So you should not be **embarrassed** of, or shy, to speak the second language. If you are speaking second language with lots of mistakes, it means that you know more than one, but it's good, it's positive. So, please, please just have the communication.

Focus 3

N: I have a project that I'm collaborating with the company in the United States and just I want to tell you that their company is located at the United States. But among the colleagues that we are collaborating, only one person is a native speaker. So this is I think the simplest example that many people in the world . . . they are speaking English as second or third language.

K: Definitely. It's even the majority. As a native English speaker, I'm a minority of the English-speaking community now. You are in the majority group. And I think it's really important to be hearing it from people like yourself to have that advice that, you know, this is going to give you the opportunity to participate on a world stage and, you know, as somebody from Iran—growing up with Farsi as a first language—coming to Japan to do the PhD and now using English globally with people on different scientific projects. It shows the power of communicative competency. It's exciting.

III. Today's Vocabulary
以下の5つの単語について辞書を読み，さまざまな用例を理解した上で，本文中での用例を日本語に訳してみましょう。

motivate
・It is her strong love of the arts that is motivating her to complete the work.
・He was motivated by a greed for fame.
What <u>motivated</u> that for her?

remain
English will <u>remain</u> as the common language for communication in science field and worldwide.
Many felt they would have a short life, or <u>remain</u> only as 'low'

colloquial speech. (Chapter 2)

The question of best practice <u>remains.</u> (Chapter 2)

particular

· He quit his job for no particular reason.

· Let's focus on this particular question.

· I made particular efforts to make my young guests feel at home.

· She is quite particular about the color of her pen.

· Your particular instructions helped me a lot in doing the work.

<u>Particular</u> languages like Chinese can play some major role in the future as well.

reverse

· I tried to reverse the direction of the discussion.

· The conclusion cannot be reversed.

· He kept walking in the reverse direction.

· The reverse side of this textile is water resistant.

It's probably hard to <u>reverse</u> that now.

embarrass

· Her straightforward questions embarrassed him.

· I am not trying to embarrass you.

I'm not <u>embarrassed</u> of mispronouncing any word.

You should not be <u>embarrassed</u> of, or shy, to speak the second language.

発展的課題

A. インタビューの中で用いられていた下記のような表現を利用しながら，あなたの専攻あるいは専門分野を英語で説明してください。

> My major is . . .
>
> my PhD is . . .
>
> I'm a material scientist . . .

B. 文法ミスや発音ミスを気にすることよりもコミュニケートしようとする姿勢のほうが大切だというナヴィッドさんの主張について，あなた自身の考えを英語または日本語で述べてください。

C. 多くの日本人が文法ミスや発音ミスを気にする理由を英語で説明してみましょう。ナヴィッドさんとクリスティーさんに説明するつもりになって，英語で話すかあるいは書いてみましょう。

【コラム】　　■■　英語が話せるようになった日　■■

　大学時代に恥ずかしい思い出があります。

　大学に入学してすぐ、「英会話」という授業をとろうと思ったのですが、最初の授業の日に教室に行ったら、いかにも英語の得意そうな顔の人たちで教室がいっぱいで、私はすっかりおじけづいて教室の入り口で引き返し、履修をやめてしまいました。

　なぜそんなに英語を話すことに苦手意識を持っていたのか、いまから振り返れば不思議です。高校を卒業する頃には、英語で分厚い小説でも普通に読んで楽しめるようにはなっていました。さらに言えば、小学校時代に1年間アメリカで暮らしたことがあり、そのときは普通にアメリカの小学校に通い、両親の通訳のようなことまでやっていました。それでも英語を話すことには、ものすごく不安を感じていました。

　ところが「英会話」の授業を取りそこなったのと同じ年のある日、アメリカのシナリオ・ライターの方とお目にかかるという、信じられないような幸運が巡ってきました。『ハリーとトント』という名作でその年のアカデミー脚本賞の候補になったジョシュ・グリーンフェルドさんです。私は映画少年以外の何者でもなかったので、もう天にも昇るほど嬉しくなって、その人と2時間くらい映画談義をしてしまいました。そのあいだに、私は英語で話すのが苦手だということをすっかり忘れてしまったようです。

　その日から英語が話せるようになりました。

　その日に何が起こったのか——私にはよくわかりません。ただ何かを伝えたい人に出会えたということは大きかったと思います。そういうときに、恥ずかしさを克服して間違いを恐れずにコミュニケートするという姿勢が自然に身につくように思えます。

（宮本陽一郎）

Part II

Lingua Franca and Diversity

Chapters 4 ～ 6

（扉）

Chapter 4

Patricia Ryan, "Don't insist on English!" (1)

(写真提供：ゲッティ イメージズ)

Patricia Ryan has spent over thirty years teaching English as a Foreign Language (EFL) in the Middle East, where she first took a job working for the British Council. In her more than three decades abroad, she has observed substantial changes in culture and language use, and she presents some of these insights in her TED talk.

[1] <u>I know what you're thinking.</u> You think I've lost my way, and somebody's going to come on the stage in a minute and guide me gently back to my seat. I get that all the time in Dubai. "Here on holiday are you, dear?" "Come to visit the children? How long are you staying?"

[2] Well actually, I hope for a while longer yet. <u>I have been living and teaching in the Gulf for over 30 years. And in that time, I have seen a lot of changes.</u> Now

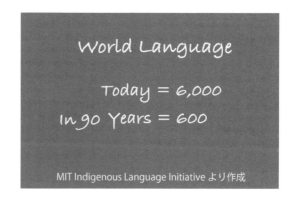

World Language

Today = 6,000
In 90 Years = 600

MIT Indigenous Language Initiative より作成

that statistic is quite shocking. And I want to talk to you today about language loss and the globalization of English. I want to tell you about my friend who was teaching English to adults in Abu Dhabi. And one fine day, she decided to take them into the garden to teach them some nature vocabulary. But it was she who ended up learning all the Arabic words for the local plants, as well as their uses—medicinal uses, cosmetics, cooking, herbal. How did those students get all that knowledge? Of course, from their grandparents and even their great-grandparents. It's not necessary to tell you how important it is to be able to communicate across generations.

[3] But sadly, today, languages are dying at an **unprecedented rate.** A language dies every 14 days. Now, at the same time, English is the **undisputed** global language. Could there be a connection? Well I don't know. But I do know that I've seen a lot of changes. When I first came out to the Gulf, I came to Kuwait in the days when it was still a hardship post. Actually, not that long ago. That is a little bit too early[1]. But nevertheless, I was recruited by the British Council[2], along with about 25 other teachers. And we were the first non-Muslims to teach in the state schools[3] there in Kuwait. We were brought to teach English because the government wanted to modernize the country and to **empower** the citizens through education. And of course, the U.K. **benefited** from some of that lovely oil wealth.

[4] Okay. Now this is the major change that I've seen—how teaching English has morphed[4] from being a mutually **beneficial** practice to becoming a massive international business that it is today. No longer just a foreign language on the school curriculum, and no longer the sole domain of mother England, it has become

---

1）実際の映像ではここでクウェートの街の様子を写した写真が出るのだが、それがかなり昔の写真であるため、このように言及しているものと思われる。

2）「文化交流と教育機会を促進する英国の公的な国際文化交流機関」であり、「文化芸術、教育、英語を通じて、英国とその他の国の人々の間につながりを育み、理解と信頼を築くために活動して」いる。

⟨https://www.britishcouncil.jp/⟩

3）公立学校。この state は「国、国家」の意味。

4）変身する

a bandwagon[5] for every English-speaking nation on earth. And why not? After all, the best education—according to the latest World University Rankings—is to be found in the universities of the U.K. and the U.S. So everybody wants to have an English education, naturally. But if you're not a native speaker, you have to pass a test.

[5] <u>Now can it be right to reject a student on linguistic ability alone?</u> Perhaps you have a computer scientist who's a genius. Would he need the same language as a lawyer, for example? Well, I don't think so. We English teachers reject them all the time. We put a stop sign, and we stop them in their tracks. They can't pursue their dream any longer, 'til they get English. Now let me put it this way: if I met a monolingual Dutch speaker who had the cure for cancer, would I stop him from entering my British University? I don't think so. But indeed, that is exactly what we do. We English teachers are the gatekeepers[6]. And you have to satisfy us first that your English is good enough. Now it can be dangerous to give too much power to a narrow segment of society. Maybe the barrier would be too universal.

[6] Okay. "But," I hear you say, "what about the research? It's all in

---

5）（政治運動・競争などで）優勢な側、人気のある側。〔新英和大辞典〕もとはパレードの先頭を行く楽隊車を指す語。
6）門番、守衛。日本語ではかなり限定的な意味で「ゲートキーパー」という語が使われることがあるが、原義を押さえておくことは重要。

English." So the books are in English, the journals are done in English, but that is a self-fulfilling prophecy[7]. It feeds the English requirement. And so it goes on. <u>I ask you, what happened to translation?</u> If you think about the Islamic Golden Age [8], there was lots of translation then. They translated from Latin and Greek into Arabic, into Persian, and then it was translated on into the Germanic languages of Europe [9] and the Romance languages[10]. And so light shone upon the Dark Ages[11] of Europe. Now don't get me wrong; I am not against teaching English, all you English teachers out there. I love it that we have a global language. We need one today more than ever. But I am against using it as a barrier. Do we really want to end up with 600 languages and the main one being English, or Chinese? We need more than that. Where do we draw the line? This system equates intelligence with a knowledge of English, which is quite **arbitrary**.

7）それを言ったこと自体がもとで結果的に的中する予言、予想。〔新英和大辞典〕
8）イスラーム黄金時代。8 世紀から 13 世紀半ばまでのアッバース朝時代を指す。学問が非常に重視され、世界各地の智が集められてアラビア語に翻訳され、そこからさまざまな言語に翻訳されていった。
9）ヨーロッパのゲルマン語系の言語といえば、ドイツ語、オランダ語、スカンジナビア諸語（フィンランド語は含まれない）が代表的。
10）スペイン語、イタリア語、ルーマニア語などがロマンス語系。
11）暗黒時代。西ローマ帝国の滅亡（476 年）から紀元 1000 年頃までのヨーロッパ中世初期の期間を知的暗黒時代と考えたことによる；時に文芸復興期までのヨーロッパ中世全体を指す。〔新英和大辞典〕

I. Understanding the Contents

下線を施した各パラグラフのトピック・センテンスを注意深く読み，それ以外は速読して，問1～5に入る内容を，それぞれ選択肢 a ～ d の中から選びましょう。

問1　パトリシア・ライアンさんの職業は……
 a. 主婦
 b. 外交官
 c. 英語教員
 d. 言語学者

問2　パトリシア・ライアンさんは中東に……
 a. 今回初めて来た
 b. 実際に住んだことはない
 c. 30 年以上前に住んでいたことがある
 d. 30 年以上にわたり住んでいる

問3　パトリシア・ライアンさんの論題は……
 a. グローバル化による社会変化
 b. 言語の喪失と英語のグローバル化
 c. 中東社会における経済的格差
 d. 中東における言語教育の進歩

問4　第2パラグラフで語られている友人の体験は……
 a. 中東で英語がどれほど一般化しているかを示すものである。
 b. 中東の人たちの植物に関する知識の豊かさを示すものである。

c. 中東の人たちが植物の名前さえ母語では覚えなくなったことを示すものである。

d. 中東の人たちが母語を通じて祖先の知識を受け継いでいることを示すものである。

問5　第5パラグラフ冒頭の "Now can it be right to reject a student on linguistic ability alone?" という問いかけに対するパトリシア・ライアンさんの答えは？

a. 語学力による入学者選別は非生産的である。

b. 英語教員は強い使命感を持って語学力による入学者選別にあたるべきである。

c. 語学試験が公正に行われている限りにおいては，それは正しいことである。

d. 英語が国際共通語となった現在，語学力による入学者選別はいたしかたのないことである。

II. The Opinions

プレゼンテーションの中の次の2つの部分を精読し，著者の主張をそれぞれ100字程度にまとめましょう。

Focus 1

But sadly, today, languages are dying at an unprecedented rate. A language dies every 14 days. Now, at the same time, English is the undisputed global language. Could there be a connection? Well I don't know. But I do know that I've seen a lot of changes. When I first came out to the Gulf, I came to Kuwait in the days when it was still a hardship post. Actually, not that long ago. That is a little bit too early. But nevertheless, I was recruited by the British Council, along with about 25 other teachers. And we were the first non-Muslims to teach in the state schools there in Kuwait. We were brought to teach English because the government wanted to modernize the country and to empower the citizens through education. And of course, the U.K. benefited from some of that lovely oil wealth.

Focus 2

Now don't get me wrong; I am not against teaching English, all you English teachers out there. I love it that we have a global language. We need one today more than ever. But I am against using it as a barrier. Do we really want to end up with 600 languages and the main one being English, or Chinese? We need more than that. Where do we draw the line? This system equates intelligence with a knowledge of English, which is quite arbitrary.

III. Today's Vocabulary

以下の5つの単語について辞書を読み, さまざまな用例を理解した上で, 本文中での用例を日本語に訳してみましょう。

unprecedented ← precede
· Thunder preceded the rain.
· Safety precedes all other concerns.

· An introduction should precede the main text.

· The number of casualties in the accident was unprecedented.

Languages are dying at an <u>unprecedented</u> rate.

undisputed ← dispute

· We disputed over the measures to be taken.

· There is a dispute over its historical explanation.

· He disputed the decision with all his might.

· Her ability is undisputed.

English is the <u>undisputed</u> global language.

empower ← power

· He empowered her to make the necessary decisions for him.

· She is not empowered to make all his wishes come true.

· This machine is powered by the wind.

The government wanted to modernize the country and to <u>empower</u> the citizens through education.

benefit (v.), beneficial ← benefit (n.)

· This program is expected to benefit everybody.

· She tried to benefit as much as she could from the experience.

· The relationship was beneficial to both parties.

· All the hard training was for your benefit.

The U.K. <u>benefited</u> from some of that lovely oil wealth.

Teaching English has morphed from being a mutually <u>beneficial</u> practice to becoming a massive international business.

arbitrary

・The distinction between the two groups was arbitrary.

・She made arbitrary claims to the shop owner.

・In a democratic society, an arbitrary government would not be tolerated.

This system equates intelligence with a knowledge of English, which is quite <u>arbitrary</u>.

発展的課題

A. これからの90年のあいだに, 地球上の言語が6,000か国語から600か国語に減少したとしたら, 本文中で述べられていること (祖先から子孫への知識の伝達) 以外に, どのような問題が生じると考えられますか?

B. 初等教育から大学院教育まで, ほぼ母語のみで提供されている日本の教育システムの長所と短所について考えてみましょう。

C. 第5パラグラフ冒頭の "Now can it be right to reject a student on linguistic ability alone?" という問いかけに対するあなた自身の答えを, 本文中に出てきた下記のような表現を可能な限り利用しながら述べてみましょう。

how important it is to be able to communicate across generations [2]

reject a student on linguistic ability alone [5]

They can't pursue their dream any longer, 'til they get English. [5]

I love it that we have a global language. [6]

We need [a global language] today more than ever. [6]

This system equates intelligence with a knowledge of English . . . [6]

I am not against . . . [6]

But I am against . . . [6]

Now don't get me wrong . . . [6]

【コラム】　■■　The History of TED Talks: Part I　■■

TED Talks have become increasingly popular in recent years. They are used by instructors in teaching contexts, are educational online resources for learners, and are enjoyed by many YouTube viewers looking for information and entertainment on the Internet. But where did TED Talks come from, and how did they become so popular?

TED Talks origins
It may be difficult to imagine, but TED Talks are older than the World Wide Web. According to Dave Roos (2015), the first TED Event occurred in 1984 in Monterrey, California, and it was the brainchild of Richard Saul Wurman, a wealthy and forward-thinking architect. The acronym, TED, stands for the three areas of **technology, entertainment**, and **design**, and Wurman was looking to change the way that public speakers spoke to their audiences. He was interested in hosting and supporting talks that differed from traditional presentations, and wanted to encourage speakers to engage their audience with interesting talks and simple, clear slideshows. He managed to promote these 'anti-conference' presentations for over fifteen years, and then he decided to sell the TED rights to a nonprofit organization called the Sapling Foundation, led by Chris Anderson, in 2001.

TED Talks structure
Although TED Talks were originally designed to last approximately 18 minutes in length (the supposed duration of the human attention span),

there are now thousands of talks available on YouTube and the TED website that last anywhere from 3 minutes to well over 20 minutes. They range in tone from instructional, to inspirational, to comedic, and speakers come from varied backgrounds in age, education, and experience. On the TED website, they organize past videos according to subjects—such as Technology, Science, Design, Social Change, The Environment, Identity, and Community, amongst others—and according to playlists that connect with topical issues, most popular talks, and other categories that nicely link together. There is also a whole library of TED-Ed videos, designed for students and instructors where they can share TED Talk ideas and connect with animators who may be able to bring their ideas to life in slides and videos.

(Kristie Collins)

References: Dave Roos "How TED Talks Work" 27 July 2015. HowStuff Works.com. <https://people.howstuffworks.com/ted-talks.htm> 5 June 2021

Chapter 5
Patricia Ryan, "Don't insist on English!" (2)

▲ Heroes Award を受賞したケニアの少年　Evans Wadongo 少年
（写真提供：ゲッティ イメージズ）

Patricia Ryan, a UK-born educator who lives and works in the United Arab Emirates (UAE), presents some of the pitfalls that may come about with the loss of languages that is currently happening worldwide. While many benefits may arise from the adoption of English as a Global Language, Ryan's talk warns of the dangers we face in losing a multitude of rich cultures linked to other languages should we insist on people using only English in the future.

[1] <u>And I want to remind you that the giants upon whose shoulders today's intelligentsia stand [1] did not have to have English, they didn't have to pass an English test.</u> Case in point [2], Einstein. He, by the way, was considered remedial at school because he was, in fact, dyslexic [3]. But fortunately for the world, he did not have to pass an English test. Because they didn't start until 1964 with TOEFL [4], the American test of English. Now it's exploded. There are lots and lots of tests of English. And millions and millions of students take these tests every year. Now you might think, you and me, "Those fees aren't bad, they're okay," but they are **prohibitive** to so many millions of poor people. So immediately, we're rejecting them.

---

1) Stand on the shoulders of giants「巨人の肩の上に立つ」のもじり。Stand on the shoulders of giants という言葉自体は小人が巨人の肩の上に乗ることによってより遠くを見渡せるという趣旨。ニュートンが友人のハレーに宛てた手紙の中で "If I have seen further, it is by standing upon the shoulders of giants." と書いたのが有名。〈https://www.bbc.co.uk/worldservice/learningenglish/movingwords/short-list/newton.shtml〉

2) 適例、例証

3) 失読症の人。ディスレクシアとは知的能力や知覚能力には異常がないにもかかわらず文字の読み書きが困難になる障がいであり、学習障がいの一種とされる。

4) アメリカの NPO である Educational Testing Service が主催している Test of English as a Foreign Language の略。ほとんどのアメリカの大学は入学しようとする外国人に受験を課している。受験料は国によって異なるが、日本では 2021 年 2 月時点で $245。

〈https://v2.ereg.ets.org/ereg/public/testcenter/availability/seats?_p=TEL〉

[2] It brings to mind [5] a headline I saw recently: "Education: The Great Divide." Now I get it, I understand why people would want to focus on English. They want to give their children the best chance in life. And to do that, they need a Western education. Because, of course, the best jobs go to people out of the Western universities, that I put on earlier. It's a circular thing.

[3] Okay. Let me tell you a story about two scientists, two English scientists. They were doing an experiment to do with [6] genetics and the forelimbs and the hind limbs of animals. But they couldn't get the results they wanted. They really didn't know what to do, until along came a German scientist who realized that they were using two words for forelimb and hind limb, whereas genetics does not **differentiate** and neither does German. So bingo [7], problem solved. If you can't think a thought, you are stuck. But if another language can think that thought, then, by cooperating, we can achieve and learn so much more.

[4] My daughter came to England from Kuwait. She had studied science and mathematics in Arabic. It's an Arabic-medium school [8]. She had to translate it into English at her grammar

---

5)（物・事が）〜を思い出させる

6 ）〜を扱う

7 ）やったあ、できた、あーら不思議、これは驚き〔リーダーズ英和辞典〕。ビンゴ ゲームでは然るべきコマが揃った人が "Bingo !" と言って勝ち名乗りを上げる。

8 ）アラビア語で教育を行う学校。Medium は medium of education の意。

school [9]. And she was the best in the class at those subjects. Which tells us that when students come to us from abroad, we may not be giving them enough **credit** for [10] what they know, and they know it in their own language. When a language dies, we don't know what we lose with that language.

[5] This is—I don't know if you saw it on CNN recently—they gave the Heroes Award to a young Kenyan shepherd boy who couldn't study at night in his village, like all the village children, because the kerosene lamp, it had smoke and it damaged his eyes. And anyway, there was never enough kerosene, because what does a dollar a day buy for you? So he invented a cost-free solar lamp. And now the children in his village get the same grades at school as the children who have electricity at home. [11] When he received his award, he said these lovely words: "The children can lead Africa from what it is today, a dark continent, to a light continent." A simple idea, but it could have such far-reaching **consequences**.

[6] People who have no light, whether it's physical or metaphorical, cannot pass our exams, and we can never know what they know. Let us not keep them and ourselves in the dark. Let us **celebrate** diversity. Mind your language. Use it to spread great ideas.

[7] Thank you very much.

---

9) イギリスでは中学校を指す。アメリカでは小学校を指すのに使われることもあるが稀。

10)「その人の手柄とする」が原義だが、ここでは本人の能力を十分に評価していないこと。

11)〈https://edition.cnn.com/2010/LIVING/02/11/cnnheroes.wadongo/〉

I. Understanding the Contents

下線を施した各パラグラフのトピック・センテンスを注意深く読み，それ以外は速読して，問1〜5に入る内容を，それぞれ選択肢a〜dの中から選びましょう。

問1　第1パラグラフで，アインシュタインに触れている目的は……

  a. 語学テストがあったおかげで偉業を成し遂げた科学者がいたことを示すため。

  b. 語学テストでは知識の量を測ることができなかった例を示すため。

  c. TOEFLが実施される以前でも，語学と科学の両方に優れた学者がいたことを示すため。

  d. 貧困のために語学テストを受験することのできなかった偉大な科学者がいたことを示すため。

問2　第2パラグラフにある "Education: The Great Divide" という見出しが意味するのは？

  a. 国による教育格差

  b. 教育格差が貧富の格差につながること

  c. 男女のあいだの教育の格差

  d. 教育問題について激しい意見の対立が生まれていること

問3　第3パラグラフで言及されているイギリス人の科学者に関するエピソードは……

  a. 実際には英語よりもドイツ語の方が，科学的思考にマッチしていることを示している。

  b. イギリス人とドイツ人が協力できたのは，英語という国際公用語のおかげであることを示している。

c. 国際共通語がなくても科学者の協力は可能であることを示す例である。

d. それぞれの国の言語は，異なる思考の方法でもあることを示す例である。

問4　第4パラグラフで語られているパトリシア・ライアンさんの娘さんの体験が示していることは？

a. 母語以外で学ぶ生徒は，成績が示す以上に優秀でありうること。

b. 2つの言語を習得することが，数学の学力も高めること。

c. 2つの言語を学ぶことのほうが，数学を身につけることより大切であること。

d. 中東社会でも，中学・高校の数学は英語で教授されていること。

問5　第5パラグラフで述べられている安価な光発電のランプを発明したケニアの少年のエピソードは……

a. 照明の有無がいかに大きな経済格差を生んでいるかを示すものである。

b. 灯油のランプより電気のランプのほうがいかに優れているかを示すものである。

c. アフリカの教育水準が英語の採用により目覚しく向上したことを示すものである。

d. 英語以外の言語から素晴らしい発想が生まれる可能性があることを示すものである。

II. The Opinions

プレゼンテーションの中の次の3つの部分を精読し，著者の主張をそれ
ぞれ100字程度にまとめましょう。

Focus 1

It brings to mind a headline I saw recently: "Education: The Great
Divide." Now I get it, I understand why people would want to focus
on English. They want to give their children the best chance in life.
And to do that, they need a Western education. Because, of course,
the best jobs go to people out of the Western universities, that I put
on earlier. It's a circular thing.

Focus 2

Okay. Let me tell you a story about two scientists, two English
scientists. They were doing an experiment to do with genetics and
the forelimbs and the hind limbs of animals. But they couldn't get
the results they wanted. They really didn't know what to do, until
along came a German scientist who realized that they were using
two words for forelimb and hind limb, whereas genetics does not
differentiate and neither does German. So bingo, problem solved. If
you can't think a thought, you are stuck. But if another language can
think that thought, then, by cooperating, we can achieve and learn so
much more.

Focus 3

People who have no light, whether it's physical or metaphorical, cannot pass our exams, and we can never know what they know. Let us not keep them and ourselves in the dark. Let us celebrate diversity. Mind your language. Use it to spread great ideas.

III. Today's Vocabulary

以下の5つの単語について辞書を読み，さまざまな用例を理解した上で，本文中での用例を日本語に訳してみましょう。

prohibitive ← prohibit

· The jewelry is being sold at a prohibitive price.

· The authorities have prohibitive power towards civilians.

· Her father prohibited her from going to the party.

They are <u>prohibitive</u> to so many millions of poor people.

differentiate ← difference

· His unusual looks differentiated him from the rest of the group.

· There is a large difference between this side and that side.

· His proposal made a difference in people's attitudes.

They were using two words for forelimb and hind limb, whereas genetics does not <u>differentiate</u> and neither does German.

credit

· The store sells on credit.

· She was never given any credit for her input.

· His accomplishments are a credit to his family.

· I'll give credit to your statement.

· You can earn two credits for taking this course.

When students come to us from abroad, we may not be giving them enough <u>credit</u> for what they know.

consequence

· You must accept the consequences of your actions.

· The issue is of little consequence.

· Princess Diana was a person of consequence in the global campaign to ban landmines.

A simple idea, but it could have such far-reaching <u>consequences</u>.

celebrate

· We celebrated his 90th birthday last Sunday.

· The Pope celebrated a mass in a rural town today.

· Her article celebrated the equality of genders.

· The project was deemed a success, and everybody involved celebrated.

Let us <u>celebrate</u> diversity.

発展的課題

A. 第2章 "The more things change . . . "の主張と，第4・5章 "Don't insist on English!"を比較しながら，あなた自身の考えを述べなさい。

B. 国際共通語としての英語を採用するメリットと，言語の多様性を大切にすることのメリットは，具体的にどのようにすれば両立するか，あなた自身の考えを述べなさい。

C. このプレゼンテーションの中では，具体的なエピソード（イギリスの科学者のこと，娘のこと，ケニアの少年のこと）で自分の意見をわかりやすく伝える表現方法が効果的に用いられていました。下記のような表現を可能な限り利用しながら，日本語固有の思考や文化が世界に影響を与えた例を英語で説明してみましょう。

I want to remind you that . . . [1]

Case in point . . . [1]

It brings to mind . . . [2]

Let me tell you a story about . . . [5]

【コラム】 ■ ■ The History of TED Talks: Part II ■ ■

Certain TED Talks have captured the attention and imagination of the world, and many of these videos have gone viral. Whether it's because of their humor, their humanity, or their powerful message, some TED speakers really stand out from the crowd. Let's look at three of the most popular TED Talks to date.

Do schools kill creativity? (Sir Ken Robinson)

In this captivating talk, Sir Ken Robinson presents how current educational systems are failing students. Robinson uses humor and storytelling to explain how schools are overlooking a multitude of skills and talents by focusing only on academic ability. He suggests that we need to place more value on creativity and imagination, and his talk leaves us feeling optimistic and eager to take up painting or dance class.

The power of vulnerability (Brené Brown)

In this humorous and touching talk, Brené Brown shares her research on human connection and explains how vulnerability is the key to living a whole-hearted life. While we all may be frightened to open up and share our real selves with the people around us, Brown's data shows how vulnerability enables us to forge deeper relationships and to live healthier, happier lives.

What makes a happy life? Lessons from the longest study on happiness (Robert Waldinger)

In this encouraging talk, the psychiatrist Robert Waldinger explains the findings of the longest study on happiness, and offers suggestions on how we can live our best lives. Drawing upon the experiences of the research participants, Waldinger highlights the common themes that emerge from the data: it isn't wealth or fame that brings long-term happiness, it is good companions and a supportive community.

The TED Talk legacy

TED Talks have now been watched by millions of people around the world, and more than 3,000 independently organized TED Conferences are held each year. These independent events, known as TEDx Conferences, can be organized and managed by people worldwide, under the auspices of TED, with the agreement that the organizers follow the TED-approved format and guidelines, and with the understanding that conferences follow the mission to study and share 'ideas worth spreading.' Be sure to keep your eyes and ears open about upcoming TED Events—maybe you will find a conference being held in a place near you!

(Kristie Collins)

Chapter 6 — Conversation with Louis Irving

Louis Irving was born in Scotland, completing his bachelor and PhD in biology in the UK. After two years in New Zealand, he came to Japan in 2007. In 2010 he moved to the University of Tsukuba to work on a new international program aimed at increasing the number of foreign students at the university. His research focuses on factors which limit plant productivity, with the aim of producing more efficient plants to feed a growing global population. He lives with his wife and young daughter, and three lazy cats.

K: Thank you so much for coming and speaking with us today, Louis. Can you tell us a little bit about who you are and what you do?

L: Okay, my name is Louis. I am assistant professor in the College of Biology at the University of Tsukuba. I am from Scotland, but I've lived in Japan for the last 13 years and I've worked at Tsukuba since 2010. I came to Tsukuba to start our G30 program [1] which is an internationalization program aimed at increasing the number of international students studying in the university. Our goal with that program was to open degree programs which are taught in English and to attract students from all over the world.

K: Tell me, what actually led you to Japan in the first place?

L: When I was doing my PhD, I became interested in a particular protein in plant leaves called rubisco [2]. And it's the enzyme which fixes carbon dioxide in photosynthesis [3]. And it's the most abundant protein in the world. And I was very

---

1) 2009 年に設立された筑波大学の Undergraduate Program of International Social Studies の略称。「社会科学分野を中心に社会開発や情報・環境等の応用分野も対象にして、世界で生起する諸問題を的確に把握・分析・解決する能力を備え、グローバル社会の要請に対応できる国際人を養成」することを目的とし、社会学類と国際総合学類に共通の英語コースが設置されている。現在は TISS と改称されている。〈http://www.soc-int.tsukuba.ac.jp/g30.php〉

2) ルビスコ（植物の光合成における暗反応で二酸化炭素と有機物質を結合させる触媒として働く酵素）。〔ジーニアス英和大辞典〕

3) 光合成：特に植物で、二酸化炭素と水と無機塩から、太陽光線をエネルギー源とし、葉緑素などの働きで炭水化物を合成する反応。〔ランダムハウス英和大辞典〕

interested in this protein and how it influenced plant efficiency or plant productivity. And the best place in the world to study it is in Tohoku University in Sendai.

K: Okay.

L: So I wrote to the professor at Tohoku University and said, "Hey, can I come and visit you for a little while?" And he said, "Sure if you can find funding." And I wrote to my research council in the UK and said, you know, "Hey, I'd like to go and do this." They said, "Sure, here's a couple thousand pounds."

K: Wow.

L: And so I came across and it was, I think, my second time of ever being overseas.

K: That's amazing.

L: Yeah, the first time I went to Russia for a month.

K: Wow!

L: Yeah, I don't do things by half[4]. So. I came to . . . and I was in Sendai for 10 weeks and I was really nervous because I knew nothing about Japan.

K: Uh-huh.

L: This is despite the fact that I'd actually studied karate since I was 15 years old.

K: It was destiny.

L: And you know, I'd done Japanese martial arts for years, but I actually didn't really know anything about Japan. It was

---

4) do things by halves は通例否定文で使われ「中途半端に、不完全に、いい加減に」という意味。do things by half measure という言い方も「物事を中途半端に行う」という意味。

a really, really far away mysterious place and I came here and I found it such an interesting place. Everything was not quite understandable, and I really like that, you know, I liked having, I suppose, a kind of little daily challenge, learning new things about this very different culture to my own. So I did that during my PhD. After my PhD we **applied** for funding so that I could come back and do a postdoc in Japan and we didn't get it. So I actually got a job in New Zealand.

K: Oh!

L: That was my third country. So I'm going further and further away every time. And so I went to New Zealand and I worked there for two and a half years. When I was in New Zealand, the lab in Sendai sent me an email and said, "**Apply** for funding." And I came back to Japan **initially** as an English teacher working for a conversation school, R.I.P. [5]

K: Really?

L: Right. It was actually in 2007. So it was just at the time when it went bankrupt, so I worked there for six months, I got paid three times.

K: Okay, very twisty road.

L: Yeah, it's really bizarre. So I did that because there was going to be a gap between finishing my job in New Zealand and starting my position in Japan.

K: Okay.

L: So I had to **apply** for funding and there was going to be a six

---

5 ）"R.I.P." は "rest in peace"（安らかに眠れ）の略。

month or a one year gap, whatever I did. So I said, "Okay. Well, do I go back to the UK for six months or do I just go to Japan and teach English for six months and then do this?" And that was the decision I made. I was in Sendai for two years, and none of my experiments worked, everything just blew up [6], everything died. And when I was there one of my colleagues came to me one day and said, "Here's this job advertisement, you should apply for this," and I looked at it, and I said, "University of Tsukuba? Where's that?!" Never, never heard of this place before and I nearly didn't **apply**.

K: Wow.

L: Because I looked up Tsukuba online and I found out, you know, it's the Science City and there's lots of foreigners working there. And I thought, "Well, they probably already have an internal candidate." So I nearly didn't **apply**, because I thought, "I'm not going to get the job." And I put my application in the last day, and I forgot my recommendation letters. So, "Okay, it's over." A couple of months later, they called me for an interview, and I was **devastated** because I was certain I wasn't going to get the job. So I thought, "Now I need to go and buy a suit. I need to go and get, you know, Shinkansen tickets, and I'm going to have to get a hotel, and it's going to be three days, and it's just going to be a waste of time and money," and I came and I had the interview and

---

6）blow up は「爆発する」という意味でも使われるが、ここでは「ダメになる、失敗する」という意味。

they offered me the job right on the spot[7].

K: Oh, wow! That's fabulous!

L: So I was . . . yeah, it was a kind of amazing turn of events. I couldn't believe it when they were like, "We like you, and we are not interviewing anybody else." And I stood there for about three minutes, turning this over in my head. "What does that mean, exactly?" And eventually I thought, "Okay . . ."

K: That's amazing. So clearly it was in the stars. You were meant to come to Tsukuba.

L: I guess so.

I. Understanding the Contents

インタビューを速読して，問1〜5に入る内容を，それぞれ選択肢a〜dの中から選びましょう。

問1　ルイスさんの専門は……
　　a. 量子力学
　　b. 英語学
　　c. 教育学
　　d. 生物学

問2　ルイスさんが最初に在籍した日本の大学は……
　　a. 北海道大学
　　b. 東北大学

7）即座に、すぐその場で

　c. 筑波大学

　d. 東京大学

問3　その次にルイスさんが滞在した国は……

　a. スコットランド

　b. ロシア

　c. オーストリア

　d. ニュージーランド

問4　ルイスさんの日本での最初の仕事は……

　a. 空手の師範

　b. 留学プログラムの統括者

　c. 英会話学校の教員

　d. 研究所勤務

問5　ルイスさんが日本の大学の G30 プログラムの教員公募に応募したとき……

　a. 面接を受けたのはルイスさんひとりだけで，その場で採用された。

　b. つくば市在住の外国人が驚くほどたくさん面接に来ていた。

　c. 応募書類を送っただけで，折り返し採用通知が届いた。

　d. 面接の際，採用はおそらく無理だと言われて諦めかけていた。

II. The Opinions

インタビューの中の次の3つの部分を精読し，Louis さんの主張をそれぞれ 100 字程度にまとめましょう。

Focus 1

The world is going through a lot of changes because of coronavirus and many other things. But Japan is an aging society, it's the oldest society on earth, and this means when you've got a shrinking population of young people then that has **implications** for universities first of all, but then also for  society as a larger thing, you know. You have more old people who need hospitals and doctors and social security, and you've got a shrinking workforce, and an aging workforce. So Japan is coming under increasing pressure in these ways. And I think that it's important for Japanese people to be able to become part of a bigger world for young people, to be able to go and study overseas, or for Japan to be able to welcome foreign people to work here.

Focus 2

. . . If you told me when I was 15 years old, "Louis, one day you will live in Japan and you know you will work at a Japanese university, you will own a house in Japan, you will have a wife and a child." If you'd told me these things that actually happened to me, I would have laughed at you. I would have thought you are insane. And I look back at me when I was young and, you know, I wasn't a bad guy at all, but I was so narrow-minded. My world was so tiny. And traveling and meeting people from around the world has just widened my world. It's made it so much bigger and so much better and my life is something I could not have imagined when I was 15 or 16 years old. So learning different languages, traveling, living different places, is **invaluable**. It's amazing. Everyone should do it.

Focus 3

We can't describe colors that we don't have a word for. We can't imagine colors we don't have a word for. We're limited by the language that we have, always, and there are words which exist in Japanese which don't exist in English because there are concepts which exist in Japan which we don't have in Western countries. And the same is true the other way around. So language and culture  are incredibly tied together. You can't understand Japan without understanding Japanese and I'm not sure that you can understand the UK or America or Australia if you don't speak English, at least to some level.

III. Today's Vocabulary

以下の5つの単語について辞書を読み，さまざまな用例を理解した上で，本文中での用例を日本語に訳してみましょう。

apply

・I am applying for this position.

・He applied his mind to how the business could make money.

・The rule does not apply here.

・The authorities are applying the same principle to this issue.

・A new name was applied to the new product.

・Apply pressure to the wound so that it will stop bleeding.

After my PhD we applied for funding.

I nearly didn't apply.

initially ← initial

・The initial impression I had of her turned out to be inaccurate.

・The reaction was initially very good.

I came back to Japan initially as an English teacher.

devastate

・The natural disaster had devastated the city a year before.

I was devastated because I was certain I wasn't going to get the job.

implication

・This new law might have a serious implication for the future.

・The implication was that we have a duty to support the project.
・Her parents, and her siblings by implication, would benefit from her success.

When you've got a shrinking population of young people, then that has <u>implications</u> for universities first of all.

invaluable

・He says that her words were invaluable when making the choice.

Learning different languages, traveling, living different places, is <u>invaluable</u>.

発展的課題

A.　あなたが英語を学ぶ動機は何ですか?

B.　日本のある小さな地方都市で暮らしている高校生のAさんの生活は,当面日本語オンリーで,将来海外で生活することなど考えたこともありません。まるで少年時代のルイスさんのようです。Aさんに英語を学ぶ意義を実感してもらうためには,どうしたらよいでしょう。

C.　あなたの受験や就職活動の思い出を,本文中の表現を利用しながら,ユーモアを交えて英語で語ってみましょう。(フィクションであっても構いません。)

【コラム】　■ ■　コミュニケーション能力　■ ■

　企業が新入社員に求めるものの最上位が「コミュニケーション能力」だと言われるようになって久しいですが、そこで求められているのはどのような能力なのでしょうか。「説得力のあるプレゼンテーションができること」「顧客のニーズを把握してそれに的確に答えること」「企業活動に必要な言葉（自社製品の説明に必要な語彙や敬語など）を正しく使えること」というあたりが一般的なイメージなのかなと想像しています。一方、言語教育で「コミュニケーション能力」を捉える場合は、もう少し違った角度からの見方があるように思います。

　言語教育の分野では「コミュニケーション能力」を4つの側面に分けて考える考え方があります。第1の側面は、文法的に正しい文が組み立てられるかどうか、という面です。たとえば、日本語と英語とでは基本的な語順が違いますが、単語だけ英語に置き換えて日本語の語順で文を組み立てようとしてもうまく伝わらないことが多く、単語を英語に置き変えた上でしかるべき語順に変えて文を組み立てた方が伝わりやすいわけで、それができるか、というのがこの第1の側面です。第2の側面は、社会言語学的にしかるべき場面でしかるべきことが言えるかどうか、という面です。例えば誰かに何かを依頼する場合に、相手に失礼でない言い方ができるかどうか、ということが問われる面です。第3の側面は、伝えることが全体として整合性を持つか（意味を成すか）、という面です。例えば一文ごとにバラバラな話題を出してしまうと、話全体としては何が言いたいのかわかりにくくなります。自分の前の発言との関連がわかるような形で次の発言を繋いでいく方が全体として何が言いたいか伝わりやすくなるわけで、それをすることができるか、という点を問題にする側面です。そして最後の側面は相手に伝えようとしたことがうまく伝わらなかった時にどうするか、という面で、例えば言い方を変えて言い直してみる、わからない単語を相手に聞く、などの方略を適切にとれるかどうかが関わってきます。

　このように見てみると、文法的に正しいかどうかという点は、こちらの言いたいことを相手に伝えるための一部でしかない、と考えることができます。それよりも、そもそも相手に伝えたいと思う事柄を持っているか、そしてそれを伝えようとする熱意があるかどうか、さらにはうまく伝わらなかった時に諦めずにやり取りを続けようとする気持ちを持ち続けることができるか、ということの方が、やり取りを行うためには本質的に重要なことであるように思えます。「グローバル英語」の時代に、どのような形の英語が求められるようになっても、伝えたいと思う内容と気持ちが必要だという点は、きっと変わらないだろうと思います。

（大橋理枝）

Part III

Lingua Franca and Multilingualism

Chapters 7 ～ 9

（扉）

Chapter 7

Lera Boroditsky,
"How language shapes the way we think" (1)

（写真提供：TED）

Lera Boroditsky is a Stanford-educated cognitive scientist and professor, currently teaching and researching at University of California, San Diego (UCSD). Born in Belarus, Lera and her family emigrated to the United States when she was twelve years old, at which point Lera learned English as her fourth language.

[1] <u>So, I'll be speaking to you using language . . . because I can</u>. This is one of these magical abilities that we humans have. We can **transmit** really complicated thoughts to one another. So what I'm doing right now is, I'm making sounds with my mouth as I'm exhaling. I'm making tones and hisses and puffs, and those are creating air vibrations in the air. Those air vibrations are traveling to you, they're hitting your eardrums, and then your brain takes those vibrations from your eardrums and transforms them into thoughts. I hope.

[2] I hope that's happening. <u>So because of this ability, we humans are able to **transmit** our ideas **across** vast reaches of space and time</u>. We're able to **transmit** knowledge **across** minds. I can put a bizarre new idea in your mind right now. I could say, "Imagine a jellyfish waltzing in a library while thinking about quantum mechanics." Now, if everything has gone relatively well in your life so far, you probably haven't had that thought before. But now I've just made you think it, through language.

[3] Now of course, there isn't just one language in the world, there are about 7,000 languages spoken around the world. And all the languages differ from one another in all kinds of ways. Some languages have different sounds, they have different vocabularies, and they also have different structures—very importantly,

different structures. <u>That begs the question</u> [1] : <u>Does the language</u>
<u>we speak shape the way we think?</u> Now, this is an ancient
question. People have been **speculating** about this question
forever. Charlemagne, Holy Roman emperor [2] , said, "To have a
second language is to have a second soul"—strong statement
that language crafts reality. But on the other hand, Shakespeare
has Juliet say [3] , "What's in a name? A rose by any other name
would smell as sweet." Well, that **suggests** that maybe language
doesn't craft reality. These arguments have gone back and forth
for thousands of years. But until recently, there hasn't been any
data to help us decide either way. Recently, in my lab and other
labs around the world, we've started doing research, and now we
have actual scientific data to weigh in on this question.

[4] <u>So let me tell you about some of my favorite examples</u>. I'll start
with an example from an Aboriginal [4] community in Australia
that I had the chance to work with. These are the Kuuk
Thaayorre people. They live in Pormpuraaw at the very west

---

1) 疑問を引き起こす。当然〜という疑問が浮かぶ。
2) カール大帝 (742-814)。768 年からフランク王国の王であり、800 年からは神聖
ローマ帝国のカール一世として君臨。
3)「シェイクスピアはジュリエットに言わせている」ということ。この have は「〜
に…をさせる」という意味。
4)「オーストラリア原住民の」。オーストラリア以外の文脈では民族や植物がその
土地にもとから存在するという意味で使われる。

edge of Cape York [5]. And what's cool about Kuuk Thaayorre [6] is, in Kuuk Thaayorre, they don't use words like "left" and "right," and instead, everything is in cardinal [7] directions: north, south, east and west. And when I say everything, I really mean

5）オーストラリア東北部にある半島の西側の地域。

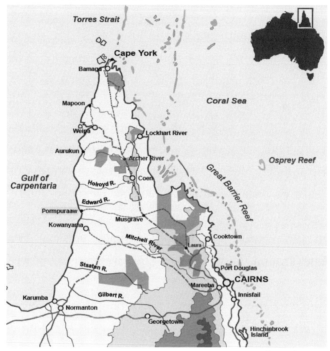

（ウィキペディアより）
〈https://upload.wikimedia.org/wikipedia/commons/c/cb/A2015_Cape_York_
Peninsula_map.svg〉

6）Austlang によれば、2016 年の時点での国勢調査による話者数は 205 人。
〈https://collection.aiatsis.gov.au/austlang/language/y69〉

7）cardinal は「基本的な、根本的な」という意味。Cardinal number は「基数」（順序ではなく量を表す数）という意味で使われる。 cardinal direction は「方位」の意。

everything. You would say something like, "Oh, there's an ant on your southwest leg." Or, "Move your cup to the north-northeast a little bit." In fact, the way that you say "hello" in Kuuk Thaayorre is you say, "Which way are you going?" And the answer should be, "North-northeast in the far distance. How about you?"

[5] <u>So imagine as you're walking around your day, every person you greet, you have to report your heading direction</u>. That would actually get you oriented pretty fast, right? Because you literally couldn't get past [8] "hello," if you didn't know which way you were going. In fact, people who speak languages like this stay oriented really, really well. They stay oriented better than we used to think humans could. We used to think that humans were worse than other creatures because of some biological excuse: "Oh, we don't have magnets in our beaks or in our scales." No; if your language and your culture trains you to do it, actually, you can do it. There are humans around the world who stay oriented really well.

[6] <u>And just to get us in agreement about how different this is from the way we do it, I want you all to close your eyes for a second and point southeast</u>. Keep your eyes closed. Point. OK, so you can open your eyes. I see you guys [9] pointing there, there, there, there, there . . . I don't know which way it is myself—

---

8)「こんにちは」に当たる挨拶すらできない。
9)「あなたたち」という意味で男性だけでなく男女のグループや女性だけのグループにも用いられる。

you have not been a lot of help. So let's just say the accuracy in this room was not very high. This is a big difference in cognitive ability **across** languages, right? Where one group—very **distinguished** group like you guys—doesn't know which way is which, but in another group, I could ask a five-year-old and they would know.

[7] <u>There are also really big differences in how people think about time.</u> So here I have pictures of my grandfather at different ages. And if I ask an English speaker to organize time, they might lay it out this way, from left to right. This has to do with writing direction. If you were a speaker of Hebrew or Arabic, you might do it going in the opposite direction, from right to left.

[8] <u>But how would the Kuuk Thaayorre, this Aboriginal group I just told you about, do it?</u> They don't use words like "left" and "right." Let me give you a hint. When we sat people facing south, they organized time from left to right. When we sat them facing north, they organized time from right to left. When we sat them facing east, time came towards the body. What's the pattern? East to west, right? So for them, time doesn't actually get locked on the body at all, it gets locked on the landscape. So for me, if I'm facing this way, then time goes this way, and if I'm facing this way, then time goes this way. I'm facing this way, time goes this way—very egocentric of me to have the

direction of time chase me around every time I turn my body[10]. For the Kuuk Thaayorre, time is locked on the landscape. It's a dramatically different way of thinking about time.

[9] Here's another really smart human trick. <u>Suppose I ask you how many penguins are there</u>[11]. Well, I bet I know how you'd solve that problem if you solved it. You went, "One, two, three, four, five, six, seven, eight." You counted them, right? You named each one with a number, and the last number you said was the number of penguins. Now, this is a little trick that you're taught to use as kids. You learn the number list and you know . . . you learn how to **apply** it. A little linguistic trick. Well, some languages don't do this, because some languages don't have exact number words. There're languages that don't have a word like "seven" or a word like "eight." And, in fact, people who speak these languages don't count, and they have trouble keeping track of exact quantities. So, for example, if I ask you to match this number of penguins to the same number of ducks, you would be able to do that by counting. But folks who don't have that linguistic trick can't do that.

---

10) 実際の動画では、話者が東を向いていれば時系列は北から南に向くことになり、話者が南を向いていれば時系列は東から西に向くことになる、ということを実演して示している。

11) TED の動画ではここでペンギンが何羽か写っている写真が表示されている。

I. Understanding the Contents

下線を施した各パラグラフのトピック・センテンスを注意深く読み，それ以外は速読して，問 1 ～ 5 に入る内容を，それぞれ選択肢 a ～ d の中から選びましょう。

問 1　レラ・ボロディツキーさんの専門は何であると推測されますか？
- a. 生物学
- b. 地理学
- c. 人類学
- d. 認知科学

問 2　言語と時間・空間とのあいだの関係について、どのように述べられていますか？
- a. 使用言語が異なっても、時間・空間の感覚は万国共通である。
- b. 使用言語が異なれば、時間・空間の感覚も異なる。
- c. 時間・空間の感覚は時代とともに変化し、それとともに言語も必ず変化する。
- d. 時間・空間の感覚が共通していれば、国際公用語は習得可能である。

問 3　オーストラリアのクウク・サアヨッレ人の方向感覚は……
- a. 左右よりも前後の関係を重視する。
- b. 前後よりも左右の関係を重視する。
- c. 前後左右の関係ではなく、東西南北の方位のみで成り立っている。
- d. 前後左右の関係も東西南北の方位も、すべて時間の感覚に置き換えられる。

問4　クウク・サアヨッレ人は，同一人物の異なる年齢の写真をどのように並べると推測できますか？
  a. 年齢順に左から右に並べる。
  b. 年齢順に右から左に並べる。
  c. 年齢順に、東から西に向かって並べる。
  d. 円環状に並べ、年齢の順序を示さない。

問5　最後のパラグラフで、ペンギンの数え方の事例に言及しているのは……
  a. 数を数えるという行為すら、言語に基づく行為であることを示すため。
  b. ペンギンの数が奇数か偶数かを、区別する言語としない言語があることを示すため。
  c. たとえ何匹いるかという結論は同じでも、数える順番は使用言語によって異なることを示すため。
  d. たとえ「7」や「8」にあたる語彙を持たない言語を用いている人々でも、数学的な思考は可能であることを示すため。

II. The Opinions
プレゼンテーションの中の次の２つの部分を精読し，著者の論点をそれぞれ100字程度にまとめましょう。

Focus 1
Now of course, there isn't just one language in the world, there are about 7,000 languages spoken around the world. And all the languages

differ from one another in all kinds of ways. Some languages have different sounds, they have different vocabularies, and they also have different structures—very importantly, different structures. That begs the question: Does the language we speak shape the way we think? Now, this is an ancient question. People have been speculating about this question forever. Charlemagne, Holy Roman emperor, said, "To have a second language is to have a second soul"—strong statement that language crafts reality. But on the other hand, Shakespeare has Juliet say, "What's in a name? A rose by any other name would smell as sweet." Well, that suggests that maybe language doesn't craft reality. These arguments have gone back and forth for thousands of years. But until recently, there hasn't been any data to help us decide either way. Recently, in my lab and other labs around the world, we've started doing research, and now we have actual scientific data to weigh in on this question.

Focus 2

But how would the Kuuk Thaayorre, this Aboriginal group I just told you about, do it? They don't use words like "left" and "right." Let me give you a hint. When we sat people facing south, they organized time from left to right. When we sat them facing north, they organized time from right to left. When we sat them facing east, time came towards the body. What's the pattern? East to west, right? So for them, time doesn't actually get locked on the body at all, it gets locked on the landscape. So for me, if I'm facing this way, then time goes this way, and if I'm facing this way, then time goes this way. I'm facing this way, time goes this way—very egocentric of me to have the direction of time chase me around every time I turn my body. For the Kuuk Thaayorre, time is locked on the landscape. It's a dramatically different way of thinking about time.

III. Today's Vocabulary
以下の6つの単語について辞書を読み，さまざまな用例を理解した上で，本文中での用例を日本語に訳してみましょう。

transmit
・The pipe transmits water to each house.
・The news was transmitted by telegraph.
・The disease does not transmit between mothers and children.
・The material transmits heat very effectively.
We can transmit really complicated thoughts to one another.
Because of this ability, we humans are able to transmit our ideas across vast reaches of space and time.
We're able to transmit knowledge across minds.

speculate
・She speculated whether she should change jobs.
・I speculated that they are siblings.
・He speculated in gold trade.
People have been speculating about this question forever.

suggest
- I suggested to him that we should change our plans.
- She suggested that we come up with a better scheme.
- The photograph suggests a peaceful afternoon.

That <u>suggests</u> that maybe language doesn't craft reality.

across
- There is a huge bridge across the strait.
- We sat across the table to discuss the issue.
- The contestants were called in from across the country.
- The two strips of paper were placed across each other.

So because of this ability, we humans are able to transmit our ideas <u>across</u> vast reaches of space and time.

We're able to transmit knowledge <u>across</u> minds.

This is a big difference in cognitive ability <u>across</u> languages.

distinguished ← distinguish
- You must distinguish between what is acceptable and what is not.
- Can you distinguish the shape of this tiny piece of equipment?
- She can be distinguished by her fashion.
- He distinguished himself in society circles.
- We need to distinguish the different types of beer—ale, lager, pilsner, and so on.
- She became a distinguished scholar.

Where one group—very <u>distinguished</u> group like you guys—doesn't know which way is which, but in another group, I could ask a five-year old and they would know.

apply → appliance

・He bought three new electrical appliances in a day.

You learn how to <u>apply</u> it.

<u>Apply</u> for funding. (Chapter 6)

発展的課題

A． 日本語という言語は、日本人の思考をどのように特徴づけているか論じてください。

B． プレゼンテーションの中で、ある言語の中に存在する区別が別の言語の中には存在しないことがあると指摘されていました。日本語の語彙の中にある区別が英語には存在しないという例を挙げましょう。

C． B.の答えを、本文中の語彙や表現を可能な限り利用して、英語で表現してみましょう。

【コラム】　　　■ ■　「必要」な語　■ ■

　言語は思考を決定するものであるからして、言語の違いは世界の把握の仕方の違いなのか。それとも、言語は文化の影響を受けるものであるからして、言語の違いは文化の違いに過ぎないのか。——言語決定論と言語相対論の論争はいまだに決着がついていません。

　この TED Talks で Lera Boroditsky さんが出しているのは、次章で挙げられるものも含めて、いずれも言語決定論の証左になりそうな例だと言えます。言語の根本的な性質として、ある言語文化に存在しない概念については、その言語の中でその概念を表す語も存在しない、という面がある（例えば英語には「わび・さび」という概念は存在しないので「わび・さび」に当たる英語の語は存在しない）ので、例えば「右」「左」という概念がない言語文化では「右」「左」という語も存在しない、ということになります。そこから「右」「左」という語が存在しない言語文化では「右」「左」の概念もない、と論じられるわけです。

　このことを言語相対論的に考えてみると、別の側面が見えてきます。「右」「左」という語がない言語文化では「右」「左」という概念を表現する必要がなかったからその語が存在しないのだ、と考えるのが言語相対論的な考え方です。「右」「左」という語がない言語文化の人でも、「右」と「左」との違いそのものは把握できるはず（例えば「東を向いて立った時に南側に来るのが『右』、北側に来るのが『左』」などの仕方で）ので、その概念を表す語がないのはその語が必要なかっただけ（すべての方向を絶対方位で表現できるのであれば確かに左右は表現する必要がないでしょう）であって、世界に対する認知が異なっているわけではない、という捉え方になります。

　ここで私が注目したいのは、どうしてその言語では「右」「左」という表

現が必要なかったのか——逆に言えば、どうして私たちには「右」「左」という表現が必要（便利に思える）なのか——ということです。考えてみれば、「右」「左」というのは私たちの人体を基準にして考えた時の捉え方です。その意味では人間中心主義的と言えるかもしれませんし、自分の体を中心に置いて考えるということからすると個人中心主義的と言えるかもしれません。更に論を進めれば、「右」「左」のような捉え方をする言語文化というのは、人間を世界の中心に置いて身の周りを把握している文化である、と言えるかもしれません。それに対して、絶対方位で全ての方向を表す言語文化というのは、人間という存在自体を脱中心化している——人間は世界の中心ではなく、（絶対方位を持つ）世界の中の一部として存在するに過ぎないのであると考えている——と言えるかもしれません。

　方向の表し方という一点からここまで論じるのは飛躍しすぎているかもしれません。でも、「右」「左」のような、身体感覚にも関わるようなところで基本的な点の捉え方が異なるということは、何か大事な意味がありそうな気もします。だから外国語を学ぶのはおもしろい——話せるか話せないかということが些末なことに感じられるような、別レベルでの楽しみ方がありそうです。

（大橋理枝）

Chapter 8
Lera Boroditsky, "How language shapes the way we think" (2)

（写真提供：TED）

Lera Boroditsky's talk explores how the languages we speak impact on the ways that we think. Her work on cross-linguistic differences and perceptions has been influential in fields as far reaching as philosophy, psychology, anthropology, and linguistics, and it shines a light on how we can all learn new perspectives from speakers of other languages.

[1] <u>Languages also differ in how they divide up the color spectrum—the visual world.</u> Some languages have lots of words for colors, some have only a couple words, "light" and "dark." And languages differ in where they put boundaries between colors. So, for example, in English, there's a word for blue that covers all of the colors that you can see on the screen, but in Russian, there isn't a single word. Instead, Russian speakers have to differentiate between light blue, "goluboy," and dark blue, "siniy." So Russians have this lifetime of experience of, in language, **distinguishing** these two colors. When we test people's ability to perceptually **discriminate** these colors, what we find is that Russian speakers are faster across this linguistic boundary. They're faster to be able to tell the difference between a light and a dark blue. And when you look at people's brains as they're looking at colors— say you have colors shifting slowly from light to dark blue—the brains of people who use different words for light and dark blue will give a surprised reaction as the colors shift from light to dark, as if, "Ooh, something has categorically changed," whereas the brains of English speakers, for example, that don't make this categorical distinction, don't give that surprise, because nothing is categorically changing.

[2] <u>Languages have all kinds of structural quirks.</u> This is one of my favorites. Lots of languages have grammatical gender; so every noun gets assigned a gender, often masculine or feminine. And these genders differ across languages. So, for example, the

sun is feminine in German but masculine in Spanish, and the moon, the reverse. Could this actually have any **consequence** for how people think? Do German speakers think of the sun as somehow more female-like, and the moon somehow more male-like? Actually, it turns out that's the case. So if you ask German and Spanish speakers to, say, describe a bridge, like the one here[1]—"bridge" happens to be grammatically feminine in German, grammatically masculine in Spanish—German speakers are more likely to say bridges are "beautiful," "elegant" and stereotypically feminine words, whereas Spanish speakers will be more likely to say they're "strong" or "long," these masculine words.

[3] <u>Languages also differ in how they describe events, right?</u> So, you take an event like this [2], an accident. In English, it's fine to say, "He broke the vase." In a language like Spanish, you might be more likely to say, "The vase broke," or, "The vase broke itself." If it's an accident, you wouldn't say that someone did it. In English, quite weirdly, we can even say things like, "I broke my arm." Now, in lots of languages, you couldn't use that construction[3] unless you are a lunatic and you went out looking

---

1）TED の動画ではもともとの舞台背景の一部として橋が映写されている。
2）TED の動画では、美術館のようなところで壺が並べて展示されており、男性が片方の壺の写真を撮ろうとして隣の壺を倒してしまっている映像が出ている。
3）「構造」や「建造物」などさまざまな意味があるが、ここでは構文のこと。

to [4] break your arm—and you succeeded. If it was an accident, you would use a different construction.

[4] <u>Now, this has **consequences**</u>. So, people who speak different languages will pay attention to different things, depending on what their language usually requires them to do. So we [5] show the same accident to English speakers and Spanish speakers, English speakers will remember who did it, because English requires you to say, "He did it; he broke the vase." Whereas Spanish speakers might be less likely to remember who did it if it's an accident, but they're more likely to remember that it was an accident. They're more likely to remember the intention. So, two people watch the same event, witness the same crime, but end up remembering different things about that event. This has **implications**, of course, for eyewitness testimony. It also has **implications** for blame and punishment. So if you take English speakers and I just show you someone breaking a vase, and I say, "He broke the vase," **as opposed to**, I say, "The vase broke," even though you can witness it yourself, you can watch the video, you can watch the crime against the vase, you will punish someone more, you will blame someone more if I just said, "He broke it," **as opposed to**, "It broke." The language guides our reasoning about events.

4）〜しようとする

5）話し手や書き手が自身を含めた複数の人を指す時に使う使い方。ここでは必ずしも聴衆と自分という意味の「我々」ではない。

[5] <u>Now, I've given you a few examples of how language can profoundly shape the way we think, and it does so in a **variety** of ways.</u> So language can have big effects, like we saw with space and time, where people can lay out space and time in completely different coordinate [6] frames from each other. Language can also have really deep effects—that's what we saw with the case of number. Having count words [7] in your language, having number words, opens up the whole world of mathematics. Of course, if you don't count, you can't do algebra, you can't do any of the things that would be required to build a room like this or make this broadcast, right? This little trick of number words gives you a stepping stone [8] into a whole cognitive realm.

[6] <u>Language can also have really early effects, what we saw in the case of color, right?</u> These are really simple, basic, perceptual decisions. We make thousands of them all the time, and yet, language is getting in there and fussing even with these tiny little perceptual decisions that we make. Language can have really broad effects. So the case of grammatical gender may be a little silly, but at the same time, grammatical gender applies to all nouns. That means language can shape how you're thinking

---

6) coordinate には動詞として「適当な位置に置く」という意味があることを考えるとここでは「配置」という意味であることが納得できるだろう。coordinates には「座標」という意味もある。
7) 数を数えるための言葉。
8) 足掛かり

about anything that can be named by a noun. That's a lot of stuff. And finally, I gave you an example of how language can shape things that have personal weight to us—ideas like blame and punishment or eyewitness memory. These are important things in our daily lives.

[7] <u>Now, the beauty of linguistic diversity is that it reveals to us just how ingenious and how flexible the human mind is.</u> Human minds have invented not one cognitive universe, but 7,000— there are 7,000 languages spoken around the world. And we can create many more—languages, of course, are living things, things that we can hone and change to suit our needs. Now, the tragic thing is that we're losing so much of this linguistic diversity all the time. So we're losing about one language a week, and by some estimates, half of the world's languages will be gone in the next hundred years. And the even worse news is that right now, almost everything we know about the human mind and the human brain is based on studies of usually American English-speaking undergraduates at universities, right? That excludes almost all humans [9]. Right? So what we know about the human mind is actually incredibly narrow and biased, and our science

---

9）現在多くの学術研究がアメリカの大学で行われているが、特に人を対象とした研究の場合は学部の授業の中で調査への協力が呼びかけられることも多い（場合によっては「調査に参加したら1点加点」などの具体的なメリットと結びつけた形で）。そのため、アメリカ人学部学生を被験者とした調査研究に基づいて学説などが構築されることが必然的に多くなっているが、それは世界中の人々の中ではほんのわずかな集団を対象にした調査に過ぎないということ。

has to do better.

[8] I want to leave you with this final thought. I've told you about how speakers of different languages think differently, but of course, that's not about how people elsewhere think. It's about how you think. It's how the language that you speak shapes the way that you think. And that gives you the opportunity to ask, "Why do I think the way that I do?" "How could I think differently?" And also, "What thoughts do I wish to create?"

　Thank you very much.

I. Understanding the Contents

下線を施した各パラグラフのトピック・センテンスを注意深く読み，それ以外は速読して，問1〜5に入る内容を，それぞれ選択肢a〜dの中から選びましょう。

問1　青という色彩について，英語とロシア語の違いは？
　　a. 青という色彩を示す一語はそれぞれに存在するが，その範囲の中での濃淡を示す言葉は英語とロシア語では異なる。
　　b. 英語の "blue" にあたる色彩を一語で示す言葉は，ロシア語には存在しない。
　　c. 英語における青にあたる一語とロシア語における青にあたる一語では，微妙に指し示す色彩の範囲が異なる。
　　d. 英語とロシア語は非常に異なる言語であるにもかかわらず，色彩

の分類の仕方そのものは完全に一致する。

問2　言語と思考との関係についてどのように述べられていますか？
　　a. 使用言語が異なっても，ものの考え方は万国共通である。
　　b. 使用言語が異なれば，思考のしかたも異なる。
　　c. 言語は思考を表現するための道具に過ぎない。
　　d. 言語と思考は別々のものであり，両者を混同してはいけない。

問3　「橋」を指し示す名詞は……
　　a. ドイツ語では男性名詞，スペイン語では女性名詞である。
　　b. ドイツ語では女性名詞，スペイン語では男性名詞である。
　　c. ドイツ語でもスペイン語でも中性名詞である。
　　d. ドイツ語でもスペイン語でも，男性名詞・女性名詞の両方が存在する。

問4　英語の "I broke my arm." という表現は……
　　a. 骨折が自己責任であることを明示する。
　　b. 骨折が不可抗力による事故であったことを示唆する。
　　c. 自発的に自分の腕を折ったという狂気を意味する。
　　d. 他の多くの言語には見られない奇妙な表現といえる。

問5　このプレゼンテーションの中で明らかにできたことを復習している
るのは……
　　a. 第1パラグラフ
　　b. 第2～4パラグラフ
　　c. 第5～7パラグラフ
　　d. 第8パラグラフ

II. The Opinions

プレゼンテーションの中の次の2つの部分を精読し，著者の論点をそれ
ぞれ100字程度にまとめましょう。

Focus 1

Now, the beauty of linguistic diversity is that it reveals to us just
how ingenious and how flexible the human mind is. Human minds
have invented not one cognitive universe, but 7,000—there are 7,000
languages spoken around the world. And we can create many more—
languages, of course, are living things, things that we can hone and
change to suit our needs. Now, the tragic thing is that we're losing so
much of this linguistic diversity all the time. So we're losing about one
language a week, and by some estimates, half of the world's languages
will be gone in the next hundred years. And the even worse news is
that right now, almost everything we know about the human mind
and the human brain is based on studies of usually American English-
speaking undergraduates at universities, right? That excludes almost
all humans. Right? So what we know about the human mind is actually
incredibly narrow and biased, and our science has to do better.

Focus 2

I want to leave you with this final thought. I've told you about how
speakers of different languages think differently, but of course, that's
not about how people elsewhere think. It's about how you think. It's
how the language that you speak shapes the way that you think. And
that gives you the opportunity to ask, "Why do I think the way that

I do?" "How could I think differently?" And also, "What thoughts do I wish to create?"

III. Today's Vocabulary
以下の6つの単語について辞書を読み，さまざまな用例を理解した上で，本文中での用例を日本語に訳してみましょう。

distinguish
Russians have this lifetime of experience of, in language, <u>distinguishing</u> these two colors.

Where one group—very <u>distinguished</u> group like you guys—doesn't know which way is which. (Chapter 7)

discriminate
- Immigrants are often discriminated against in the host society.
- It is important to discriminate between an original piece of work and a mere copy.
- You can discriminate a helicopter from an airplane by the sound they make when they fly.

When we test people's ability to perceptually <u>discriminate</u> these colors, what we find is that Russian speakers are faster across this linguistic boundary.

consequence
Could this actually have any <u>consequence</u> for how people think?

Now, this has <u>consequences</u>.

A simple idea, but it could have such far-reaching <u>consequences</u>. (Chapter 5)

implication ← imply

· He shows his intentions only by implications.

· Her implication in the scheme was big news to all of us.

· He implied that she would not be able to do it.

· A disagreement implies a difference in opinion.

This has <u>implications</u>, of course, for eyewitness testimony.

It also has <u>implications</u> for blame and punishment.

as opposed to

· He used a taxi to go there as opposed to taking a bus.

· I chose green as opposed to purple.

I say, "He broke the vase," <u>as opposed to</u>, I say, "The vase broke."

You will blame someone more if I just said, "He broke it," <u>as opposed to</u>, "It broke."

variety

· It is a good idea to give variety to your daily schedule.

· I was amazed at the variety of textures they had prepared.

· There were varieties of opinions from the students in the class.

· A variety of fish was sold at the fisherman's market.

I've given you a few examples of how language can profoundly shape the way we think, and it does so in a <u>variety</u> of ways.

発展的課題

A．第3パラグラフで，文法構造の違いが，それぞれの言語を使用する人々の思考方法の違いに影響を与えている事例が挙げられていましたが。日本語についてそのような事例がないか考えてみましょう。

B．第8パラグラフの "How could I think differently?" という問いに，あなたならどのように答えますか？

C．日本語の「青」と英語の "blue" の違いを，本文中の表現を可能な限り利用しながら，英語で説明してみましょう。

【コラム】 ■ ■ 色の数 ■ ■

　Lera Boroditsky さんが今回取り上げたものの中で、ロシア語では区別する（即ち異なる語で表現する）「濃い青」と「薄い青」を英語では区別しない、という話がありましたが、色の区別の仕方は言語によって著しく異なります。色の名前を表す語（色彩語）がいくつあるかということと、その色彩語がいくつの分類に分けて考えられているか（例えば「紫」「青紫」「薄紫」「暗い紫」「濃い紫」「さめた紫」「ライラック色」はいずれも日本語の中にある色彩語ですが、これは2つのグループに分類されるようで、「紫」・「青紫」・「暗い紫」・「濃い紫」が同じグループ、「薄紫」・「さめた紫」・「ライラック色」は別のグループ、と分類されました）ということを、ある研究*でさまざまな言語について調査したところ、次のような結果になったようです。

言語	色彩語の数	分類数
ロシア語	296	56
フランス語	284	54
英語	279	53
ハンガリー語	187	53
セルビア語	128	52
ブルガリア語	193	51
エストニア語	158	51
日本語	118 †	46
タジク語	77	40
アムハラ語	66	39
ウズベク語	96	34
バンバラ語	46	24

† 　ただし別の文献では 267 とされている

* 　ワシレヴィチ,アレクサンドル・ペトロヴィチ（2008）／小林 潔 訳「色彩表示語彙の現代の発達傾向」三星宗雄 編著『世界の色の記号：自然・言語・文化の諸相』第2章第6節（pp.133-165）お茶の水書房、2011
　表は p.152 より転載

　ある言語の中に色彩語がいくつあるかということは、その言語文化で色をどのくらい細かく区別しているかということの目安になります（同じ色を別の言葉で表している場合もあるので、あまり単純には言えませんが）。色彩語というのは可視光線の波長のどこからどこまでを「同じ色」と捉えるか、ということを示すことにもなります。だからこそ「虹は何色<ruby>何色<rt>なんしょく</rt></ruby>？」という問いへの答えが言語によって異なることになるのです。日本語では7色とされますが、6色とする言語、5色とする言語、2色とする言語もあります。

（大橋理枝）

Chapter 9

Conversation with Xiaoyin Wang

Xiaoyin Wang formerly taught English at Soochow University in Jiangsu province, China, from which she herself graduated. Although reluctant to come to Japan 27 years ago when her husband asked her to join him at Hiroshima University, it was she who later insisted that the family remain in Tsukuba when a job offer was presented for her husband to transfer elsewhere. Fluent in English, Japanese, as well as Chinese, she first worked at Tsukuba City Hall as a Coordinator for International Relations, and, from 2016, she has been working at JISTEC, an organization that provides support services for foreign researchers in Tsukuba.

K: Alright, thank you so much, Xiaoyin, for coming and . . . and letting us interview you today.

X: Thank you for having me. Nice to see you.

K: Thank you. Likewise. Can you tell us a little bit about yourself, who you are, and what you do?

X: Okay, my name is Xiaoyin Wang. I came to Japan about 20 . . . I guess 26 or 27 years ago, in 1994, yeah, so I've been living here for that many years. And first of all, I went to Hiroshima University with my husband and I had my master's course there. And after graduation my husband had a chance to go to Canada to have his PhD studies . . . a postdoc, to study. So I went there with him and stayed for . . . for maybe half a year, but he stayed for one year. And I came back to Japan because he had a job here at Tsukuba University. So that's why I came back to Japan with my family and since then. I think it was 1998. And since then I have been staying in Tsukuba, and I love here. Yeah. I don't want to go anywhere else, yeah.

K: That's so interesting. But when you first came to Japan were you expecting to stay here and to, you know, have a life in Japan?

X: Well, honestly speaking, no. It wasn't my plan to come to Japan, actually. I had always wanted to go to a native English-speaking country because I majored in English at university, and it was like everybody's dream to want to go abroad to study at the time, you know. China had just opened to the outside world at that period of time, and I had wanted to go to either US or Canada or, you know, Britain, these places. But it so happened that my husband had a chance to study in Japan, at Hiroshima University with a math professor that he admired a lot. Yeah, PhD study, yeah. So he came here, and not long after he came here, he brought me and the kids here. So I came here. When I came here, I didn't know any Japanese. So I was like . . . oh, of course, it's not true. I knew, you know, *arigato gozaimasu* and I probably knew, yeah, *konnichiwa*, things like that, basic *aisatsu*, but I didn't know any Japanese.

K: Oh my goodness. And so you already had your girls in China? How old were the girls when you took them here?

X: They were four, maybe? Yeah, three or four years old.

K: Wow. That is a brave move, taking twin four-year-old daughters to a country where you don't speak the language. Wow. Did you enjoy it? Was it a good fit when you went to Hiroshima?

X: Well, of course it was, because, you know, I never thought about coming to Japan, but after I came to Japan—well not long—I found that this is the place for me. And I wanted to stay here longer. I wanted, you know, to know more about the people and the culture and this country. And then I just totally fell in love with this country. I didn't want to go anywhere else.

K: Oh, that's really great! So I know that you actually have become a Japanese citizen. When did you make that decision? And how did you make that decision?

X: Okay, that was about ten years ago, maybe a little more than ten years ago, before we bought our house. Because, you know, in order to take the loan, you know, mortgage, you would have to either have a Japanese citizenship or permanent resident [1]. Because we were torn in between whether to get a permanent residency or Japanese citizenship. But you know, my husband is a university professor and he has to go abroad to have, you know, joint research and meetings a lot. So if we get a permanent residency, he's still going to have a Chinese passport. And then whenever, wherever he goes, he has to take visa, and it's such a headache, you know. You have to . . . it's not only expensive, he has to go to Tokyo, he has to get interviews and stuff like that, and sometimes it takes time and the meeting will be over by the time he gets the visa. So we decided to get the citizenship, right.

K: Now, does that mean . . . are your daughters full Japanese citizens, or dual, or Chinese?

X: No, actually my daughters . . . they can apply for Japanese citizenship. They could, at the time, apply Japanese citizenship

---

1）現在の日本では法律上は外国人でも家を購入したり土地を所有したりすることが可能だが、日本の金融機関のほとんどは外国人が住宅ローンを組むための条件として永住権を持っていることを挙げているようである。〈https://magazine.aruhi-corp.co.jp/00000462/〉

with us. And actually we had prepared to that, and the documents were all ready. But in the beginning my daughters decided . . . at the time they were at the university. They were, like, thinking about this decision, and they decided to cancel that. Right, yeah, they did. But now I can tell you, one of my daughters, after she got a job in Japan, she decided to apply too. So she is now Japanese citizen. Now, the other one hasn't applied.

K: Isn't that interesting!

X: It is. Because they decided . . . they told us, "Mom, we have thought about this for a while, and it's not that we don't want to, it's just that we are too young to decide, you know, we need to have more experience and we need to know more about Japan and, you know, the pros and cons [2] about this, and we are going to decide by ourselves later." Right. So they didn't.

K: I think that's really impressive. And, interestingly, my family, we were raised with two citizenships because my parents were American and we were living in Canada. So we all had American and Canadian. And . . .

X: Dual citizenship were allowed?

K: Yep, between the US and Canada [3]. And it's just in the last

---

2) 利点と欠点。pro は「玄人」という意味の pro とは同音異義語。con も「欺く」という意味の con とは同音異義語。pros and cons という成句で使われる場合が非常に多い。

3) 在日米国大使館・領事館のウェブサイトによれば、アメリカの最高裁判所は二重国籍を「法律上認められている資格」であるとし、「二カ国での国民の権利を得、責任を負うことになる」と述べているとのことである。〈https://jp.usembassy.gov/ja/u-s-citizen-services-ja/citizenship-services-ja/dual-nationality-ja/〉

three years, four years, that my parents and I have actually officially given up our American citizenship.

X: Yeah, I heard about that.

K: But my brother remains . . . he's living in Chicago, and he has his American, so he has dual [citizenship]. But, for him, like your husband, there's reasons why it just makes more sense for traveling for business and such to have the American. So I think it's a very different world we live in now, where languages and passports and visas . . . it's a complicated, complicated situation that all of us have to think through carefully, yeah. Very cool.

Please tell me a little bit about what you do for your work here in Tsukuba.

X: Oh, okay. Well initially, I worked at Tsukuba City Hall as a translator. Actually, what they call was, when they hired me, the title for this job was called Coordinator for International Relations. Yeah, that's right. I worked at Tsukuba City Hall for about five years. And, first of all, they just wanted to hire somebody who could speak Japanese as well as English and Chinese. So because there were foreigners visiting there, and they wanted to take the procedures so they needed a translator. So initially, I was just doing the translator, translating thing. And then after that, I got more and more involved with the city, like sister city business, you know. Well, I had a chance to visit the US and Canada and Shenzhen, China. All sister cities of Tsukuba.

K: Okay, and can you tell us again? What would JISTEC [4] . . . what does that stand for?

X: Okay. JISTEC stands for Japan International Science and Technology Exchange Center.

K: What are the main responsibilities for JISTEC?

X: We can only **serve** research **institutes** that have contract with us. So, mostly researchers from foreign countries. They come here to Tsukuba to do research. They usually don't stay that long, like two or three years at most. Some people, of course, get hired by the Japanese research **institutes** and they would stay, like Navid [5]. But other people mostly just stay for a couple of years, and they have language problems. And, you know, in Japan it's quite difficult to do all these initial procedures, without some help.

K: Such as?

X: Going to city office to register your address, join the health insurance, renting an apartment, and going to hospitals, for example.

K: Yeah, it's genuinely a different experience if you have that support, and this is where having a communicative language community here, is really important.

---

4 ）科学技術国際交流センター。「科学技術分野における国内外の交流の促進、科学技術分野の研究および研究者への助成並びに科学技術分野の研究の促進を行うことにより、科学技術の振興を図るとともに、国際社会に貢献すること」を事業目的として掲げており、事業概要の4番目の項目に「内外の研究者のための生活支援」を挙げている。〈https://www.jistec.or.jp/about/〉

5 ）Chapter 3 に登場した Navid Sepehri 氏のこと。

X: Especially in the beginning.

K: Gosh, yeah. And pointing out where they might want to find support and social connections. I know that you and Anna [6] have probably been there for the birth of hundreds of babies.

X: Oh, I don't know how many people. One year [it] was like eight.

I. Understanding the Contents

インタビューを速読して，問1～5に入る内容を，それぞれ選択肢 a ～ d の中から選びましょう。

問1　シャウインさんが日本に来るきっかけとなったのは……
  a. 夫の留学
  b. 夫の日本企業への就職
  c. 自身の日本企業への就職
  d. 自身の公務員としての就職

問2　初めて来日したときのシャウインさんは……
  a. 日本語に不自由がなく，長年日本での生活を希望していた。
  b. 日本での生活は想定外で，ほとんど日本語が話せなかった。
  c. 日本での生活は想定外だったが，日本語に不自由はなかった。
  d. 日本語は不自由だったが，長年日本での生活を希望していた。

6）JISTEC を創業したシャウインさんの同僚。

問3　シャウインさんが日本国籍を取得したきっかけは……
　a. つくば市に就職するため
　b. 家を購入するため
　c. 子どもの将来のため
　d. 結婚のため

問4　シャウインさんの2人のお子さんの現在の国籍は？
　a. 2人とも日本国籍を持っている。
　b. 2人とも中国籍である。
　c. 1人は中国籍でもう1人は日本国籍である。
　d. 1人は中国籍でもう1人は二重国籍である。

問5　シャウインさんが現在勤務している JISTEC は……
　a. つくば市と姉妹都市との交流を推進する団体
　b. つくば市内の学校の英語教育を支援する団体
　c. 外国人研究者のリクルートを代行する団体
　d. 外国人がつくば市で生活を始める際の手続きなどを支援する団体

II. The Opinions

インタビューの中の次の3つの部分を精読し，シャウインさんの主張を
それぞれ100字程度にまとめましょう。

Focus 1

K: Do you feel like a person's personality and/or self-expression
changes when they shift between languages?

X: Well, actually, I don't think a person's personality can change according to what language he or she is speaking, just taking me for example. I think, whatever language I speak, I'm always me. And I'm always . . . I'm not so loud, I'm a little bit shy. If I'm with a group of people, I'm not the one who speaks a lot. So I don't think personality would change. But probably depending on what language I'm speaking, I would probably behave a little differently.

K: Can you give an example?

X: For example, if I'm having a meeting with a lot of Japanese people, and people can discuss about a topic, I would not be very active. I would not just speak up before being asked to. I would just keep quiet, mostly, because it's expected, in Japanese culture. But if I'm with a Chinese group, I will probably do whatever I want to, and speak up. And if I'm with an English-speaking group, probably that too.

Focus 2

X: [A piece of advice] to Japanese, in terms of learning languages . . . I think if you want to learn a language you have to practice, right? You have to get over your shyness at least, and don't think about perfectness. Just try to speak whatever you have learned. Try to use it, even if you are not using it in the right way. Gradually I think you will get it. Yeah, that's one thing. And if I'm a Japanese parent and I want my kid to learn a foreign language, I think . . . I would, if I had a chance, or if I have financial **resources**, I will send that kid to a native-speaking environment. Back then, we didn't have an English speaker around us, and we were listening to the tape recorders, you know.

K: Oh, I remember those days.

X: No videos, no movies, you know. Nowadays you can find whatever you want.

K: Yeah, online, or through just people in your community.

Focus 3

X: Some people [who come to Japan] would focus their attention on research. And they just try to avoid speaking to Japanese people. Some research labs are full of Chinese, for example. Even Japanese people can speak English. So they just use English. Or use their own language without using Japanese, without learning Japanese. I think it's such a **pity**. And if you are in that environment, you don't have to spend time to go abroad to learn language. You are here. Why don't you just take this great opportunity to learn the language, right?

K: And with it comes the culture and the people.

X: Right, to make friends. Making friends with Japanese people. That's basically how I learned Japanese.

K: Yeah. And I think the greatest **gift** is just that we can make friends. We can understand people so much more, the more languages we know.

X: Yeah. I just find it such an advantage to know language, different languages, to know people from different culture, you know.

K: It just makes life more rich.

X: Yeah, much more interesting.

III. Today's Vocabulary

以下の 5 つの単語について辞書を読み，さまざまな用例を理解した上で，本文中での用例を日本語に訳してみましょう。

serve

・She has been serving as a police officer for more than a decade.

・It was he who served me at the restaurant.

・A bedsheet can serve as a screen for projecting slides.

・He was able to win the tennis match today because he served well.

We can only <u>serve</u> research institutes that have contract with us.

institute

・MIT stands for Massachusetts Institute of Technology.

・The art institute is closed today.

・She went to a professional institute to deepen her knowledge.

We can only serve research <u>institutes</u> that have contract with us.

Some people of course get hired by the Japanese research <u>institutes</u>.

resource

・We must secure the water resource.

・Human resources are the most precious component of our company.

・She spent all her resources on art.

・Use all the resources available to get through this situation.

・He is a man of great resources.

If I have the financial <u>resources</u>, I will send that kid to a native-speaking environment.

pity

・What a pity that you can't come!

・She hates being helped out of pity.

・He pitied the little kitten crying in the rain and brought it home.

I think it's such a pity.

gift

・Thank you very much for the wonderful gift you gave me.

・You have a gift for music.

・She made a gift of 100 dollars for the organization.

The greatest gift is that we can make friends.

発展的課題

A．もしあなたがシャウインさんと同じように幼い子どもを連れて海外で生活することになったとしたら，あなたは家庭と学校で子どもにどのような言語を学ばせますか？またその場合のメリットとデメリットを考えてみましょう。

B．もしあなたが住んでいる市町村で多くの外国人を住民として迎える必要が生じたとしたら，住民としてどのようなことを心がけるべきでしょうか。

C．グローバル化の時代であるから準国際公用語としての英語を学習すべきだという議論と，シャウインさんの言語習得に対する考え方とのあいだには，どのような違いがあるでしょう。シャウインさんの言葉を引用しながら，英語で述べなさい。

【コラム】　■ ■　英語の栄養摂取　■ ■

　外国語を習得しようとする人間にとって、吸収しやすい栄養と吸収しづらい栄養とがあるように思えます。

　「吸収しやすい栄養」というのは、自分にとってとびきり関心のあるトピック、喉から手が出るほどに欲しい情報です。そういう素材を使って練習すれば、読み取れないことや聞き取れないことへの恐れなどふっとびます。そして情報を得るというそれだけの目的のために読み聞く——つまり普通に読む目と普通に聞く耳ができあがります。

　私自身にとっていちばんリスニング力の練習になったケースを挙げましょう。私は大学時代、なぜかアメリカン・フットボールにはまっていました。当時はアメリカのプロフットボールの試合結果をリアルタイムで知るための唯一の手段が、FEN（Far East Network、極東放送ネットワーク）の英語ラジオ放送でした。中継の中継の中継のようなかたちで届くので、ノイズだらけのひどい音声でした。

　しかしそんなことはお構いなしに、ともかく私はラジオにかじりついていました。リスニングの練習をしようなどという意識は毛頭ありませんでしたが、私の「リスニング力」は飛躍的に進歩したようです。

　「吸収しやすい栄養」というのは、英語で読んでいること、英語で聞いているということを忘れるほどに興味のある素材のことです。料理のレシピでも、映画評やコンサート評でも、なんでも構いません。

　インタビューの中でも述べられていたように、今はインターネットの時代ですから、FEN の雑音だらけの音声を聞くというような無茶をしなくても、「吸収しやすい栄養」が無尽蔵にあります。そういう栄養を毎日15分とか週に1時間とか、定期的に摂取してください。どんな授業からもこれに代わる栄養は得られません。

（宮本陽一郎）

Part IV

Glocal English

Chapters 10 ～ 13

（扉）

Chapter 10

Lionel Wee, *The Singlish Controversy* (1)

▲シンガポール国立大学キャンパス
（写真提供：ユニフォトプレス）

Lionel Wee is a Professor in the Department of English Language & Literature at the National University of Singapore. His research spans from general issues in sociolinguistics and pragmatics, to language policies, to World Englishes, particularly in relation to the Singapore context. Professor Wee served for many years on the Singapore Government's Speak Good English Movement.

[1] Several years ago, just before I was invited to become a committee member of the Singapore government's Speak Good English Movement [1] in the early 2000s, <u>I was involved in a meeting with senior civil servants [2] who were tasked with handling the Singlish [3] 'problem' and improving standards of English in Singapore</u>. The meeting took place in a small office in my Department of English Language & Literature at the National University of Singapore [4].

[2] After the meeting, I bumped into a colleague who had happened to walk past the office while the meeting was in

---

1）シンガポール人が使う英語を英語母語話者の発話形態に近づけようとする運動。シンガポールでは教育言語が英語となっており、人々は日常生活の中でも英語を使うが、例えば Singlish では使われるような "Why you so like that?" というような言い方を誤りとし、"Why are you behaving in such a manner?" を正しい形とする。〈https://www.researchgate.net/publication/287789536_The_Speak_Good_English_Movement_A_web-user's_perspective〉

2）公務員

3）シンガポールの国語はマレー語であり、公用語として英語、中国語、マレー語、タミール語が使われている。シンガポールが 1965 年にシンガポール共和国として独立した際に旧宗主国の言語である英語を公用語と定めたが、さまざまな原住民部族が自言語を混ぜた形で英語を使うようになったことから「シンガポール英語」が生まれたとされる。〈https://www.bbc.com/news/magazine-33809914〉

4）シンガポール国立大学。1905 年設立〈https://www.nus.edu.sg/about#corporate-information〉。2019 年度で学部・大学院合わせて学生数 38,415、教職員数 12,349 人〈https://www.nus.edu.sg/docs/default-source/annual-report/nus-annualreport-2020.pdf?t=NUS_AR_201007〉。Department of English Language & Literature は Faculty of Arts and Social Sciences の中にあり、Department of Philosophy、Department of History と共に Division of Humanities に入っている。

progress. She told me that she had heard shouting coming from within and wondered what the fuss was about. <u>I told her that one of the civil servants had reacted angrily when I tried to explain</u> that (i) there is no necessary correlation between the presence of Singlish and any drop in standards of English, much less[5] any evidence that the former is the cause of the latter; (ii) it is difficult, if not impossible, to ascertain with any objective certainty that standards of English are actually dropping, since the distinction between linguistic innovations and errors is a fluid one; and (iii) the global spread of English means we have to accept that there will be changes to the language as it takes root [6] in different societies and is both **adopted** and **adapted** by various users for multiple communicative purposes. The indignant civil servant found these points difficult to accept and, instead, accused me (and linguists in general) of being far too willing to **tolerate** variations in language use and therefore of irresponsibly contributing to the undesirable divergences from good/standard/proper English.

[3] <u>The heated discussion did not prevent the government from inviting me to join the Speak Good English Movement.</u> A cynical interpretation (one that is perhaps not without merit) would be that the invitation was motivated by the goal of bringing into the fold [7] and thereby co-opting potential 'troublemakers'.

5）ましてや～ない
6）定着する
7）「折る」という意味の同音異義語とは別語。共通の信念などを抱く人々の団体を指す。原義は羊の囲い・おり。

Nevertheless, I accepted the invitation because I thought it would **provide** me with a good opportunity to **engage** in extended discussions with government representatives about language matters and, specifically, about various **assumptions** concerning Singlish and Standard English.

I. Understanding the Contents

下線を施した各パラグラフのトピック・センテンスを注意深く読み，それ以外は速読して，問1〜5に入る内容を，それぞれ選択肢a〜dの中から選びましょう。

問1　第1パラグラフの目的は……
　a. 文書全体で扱う本題を明示すること
　b. 比較対象を通じて、本題を明らかにすること
　c. キーワードを定義することにより読者を本題に導くこと
　d. あるエピソードを通じて読者を本題に導くこと

問2　この文章の書き手であるライオネル・ウィー氏は……
　a. シンガポールの政府高官
　b. 大学の英文科教員
　c. 言語学者
　d. 警官

問3　Singlish とは……

　a. "Standard English" のこと

　b. シンガポール固有の英語のこと

　c. 英語を唯一のシンガポール国語とする運動のこと

　d. シンガポールのさまざまな方言の総称

問4　ライオネル・ウィー氏は……

　a. Singlish を排除し、"Standard English"の教育を推進する立場である。

　b. Singlish を排除し、伝統的なマレー語の使用を推進する立場である。

　c. Singlish に関して中立的な立場をとっている。

　d. Singlish を擁護する立場をとっている。

問5　政府がライオネル・ウィー氏を "Speak Good English Movement" の委員に選んだのは……

　a. やっかいな意見の持ち主を取り込んでしまう目的であったと推測される。

　b. 国立大学の英文科の教員であるからだったと推測される。

　c. 中立的な立場をとっている数少ない人物であったからと推測される。

　d. Singlish 批判の急先鋒であったからだったと推測される。

II. The Opinions

プレゼンテーションの中の次の2つの部分を精読し，著者の主張をそれ
ぞれ100字程度にまとめましょう。

Focus 1

After the meeting, I bumped into a colleague who had happened
to walk past the office while the meeting was in progress. She told
me that she had heard shouting coming from within and wondered
what the fuss was about. I told her that one of the civil servants
had reacted angrily when I tried to explain that (i) there is no
necessary correlation between the presence of Singlish and any drop
in standards of English, much less any evidence that the former is
the cause of the latter; (ii) it is difficult, if not impossible, to ascertain
with any objective certainty that standards of English are actually
dropping, since the distinction between linguistic innovations and
errors is a fluid one; and (iii) the global spread of English means we
have to accept that there will be changes to the language as it takes
root in different societies and is both adopted and adapted by various
users for multiple communicative purposes.

Focus 2

The heated discussion did not prevent the government from
inviting me to join the Speak Good English Movement. A cynical
interpretation (one that is perhaps not without merit) would be that
the invitation was motivated by the goal of bringing into the fold and
thereby co-opting potential 'troublemakers'. Nevertheless, I accepted

the invitation because I thought it would provide me with a good opportunity to engage in extended discussions with government representatives about language matters and, specifically, about various assumptions concerning Singlish and Standard English.

III. Today's Vocabulary

以下の６つの単語について辞書を読み，さまざまな用例を理解した上で，本文中での用例を日本語に訳してみましょう。

adopt

There will be changes to the language as it takes root in different societies and is both <u>adopted</u> and adapted by various users for multiple communicative purposes.

In 2008 I went to Australia for graduate studies and decided to <u>adopt</u> a Western name. (Chapter 1)

adapt

・He adapted to the Japanese lifestyle very quickly.

・"West Side Story" is adapted from the play "Romeo and Juliet" by Shakespeare.

・It is a good idea to adapt your presentation style to the audience.

There will be changes to the language as it takes root in different societies and is both adopted and <u>adapted</u> by various users for multiple communicative purposes.

tolerate

· Bullying shall not be tolerated.

· He could not tolerate any more misconduct.

· Several feudal lords in Japan tolerated Christianity in the 1500s.

The indignant civil servant accused me of being far too willing to tolerate variations in language use.

provide

· Transportation fees will be provided.

· She was provided with all the necessary equipment for the job.

· The contract provides that both parties make equal contributions to the project.

· The work will not be delayed, provided that the design is decided in time.

I thought it would provide me with a good opportunity to engage in extended discussions.

engage

· He is engaged in a complicated deal.

· She was engaged in an annoying phone call.

· My time is fully engaged in gym exercises.

· I was engaged with the beauty of the scenery.

· They are engaged.

I thought it would provide me with a good opportunity to engage in extended discussions.

assumption ← assume

・The figures presented here are just assumptions.

・There is great pressure arising from the assumption to the highest position.

・An investigation must not begin with the assumption of guilt.

・He assumed that she was well versed in her field.

I thought it would provide me with a good opportunity to engage in extended discussions with government representatives about language matters and, specifically, about various assumptions concerning Singlish and Standard English.

発展的課題

A．Singlish にあたるような混成英語が日本では生まれないのはなぜでしょうか？

B．シンガポールの人々はなぜ標準英語ではなく Singlish を使用するようになったのでしょうか？その動機について考えてみましょう。

C．現在身のまわりで論争となっている問題についてのあなたの立場を、本文第2パラグラフにならって3点に整理し、簡潔明瞭に英語で表現してみましょう。

【コラム】　　　■■　ワールド・ミュージック　■■

　放送授業のテーマ音楽は気に入っていただけたでしょうか？

　アメリカのギタリストであるライ・クーダーの演奏するボトルネック・ギターと、インドのギタリストのV・M・バットの演奏するモーハン・ヴィーナのコラボレーションによって生まれた名盤『ミーティング・バイ・ザ・リバー』からとっています。このアルバムは1994年に、グラミー賞の最優秀ワールド・ミュージック・アルバム賞を受賞しています。

　V・M・バットはこのアルバムについて、「音楽にあっては、宗教的な障壁も地理的な障壁も言葉の障壁もない。音楽はユニバーサルな言葉だ。私の作品「ミーティング・バイ・ザ・リヴァー」はそのことを説明しようとしたものだ」と、あるインタビューの中で述べています。「音楽はユニバーサルな言葉だ」というバットの言葉は、ある意味ではあたりまえのことを言っているようにも聞こえます。例えばモーツァルトの音楽やビートルズの音楽が国境を越えた「ユニバーサルな」音楽だと誰もが納得できるでしょう。

　しかしライ・クーダーとV・M・バットが、このアルバムで試みたことは、もう少し複雑です。アルバムの中の一曲の「ガンジス・デルタ・ブルース」というタイトルが示すように、V・M・バットが演奏するガンジス川のインド音楽と、ライ・クーダーの演奏するミシシッピー川のデルタ・ブルース——いわば2つの川がこのアルバムの中で合流してひとつの音楽空間を作ります。インド楽器を使った西欧音楽でも、西欧楽器を使ったインド音楽でもありません。

　「グローカル」という便利な言葉があります。つまりグローバルであると同時にローカルであるという意味です。このアルバムは「グローカル」な文化への憧れを体感させてくれます。

　それはこの授業の中で展開されるさまざまな議論にも合流するもので

しょう。つまりグローバル社会で共通言語で語り合う必要を感じると同時に、しかしローカルな言葉や英語のローカルな使い方も尊重したいという想いです。

（宮本陽一郎）

▲ライ・クーダイ
（写真提供：ユニフォトプレス）

▲Ｖ・Ｍ・バット
（写真提供：ユニフォトプレス）

Chapter 11 Lionel Wee, *The Singlish Controversy* (2)

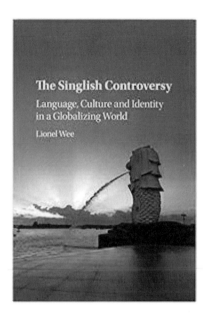

Lionel Wee's recent book, *The Singlish Controversy: Language, Culture and Identity in a Globalizing World* (2020), tackles controversial socio-political debates related to Singlish and Singapore's language policy. His work raises many interesting points on colloquial discourse, creoles, and World Englishes, and the inescapable connections between language, culture and identity in our increasingly connected world.

[1] <u>I have to say that, in retrospect, my time as a member of the Speak Good English Movement was indeed quite rewarding</u>. The other committee members with whom I had the privilege of working were often open-minded about the complexities of language. In turn, I came to be more **appreciative** of the kinds of pressures that civil servants work under and from which, as an academic, I was relatively free. For example, running an official campaign such as the Speak Good English Movement meant being answerable to politicians and members of the public about how resources were being spent and having to show that some 'progress' was being made each year (such as reducing the rampant use of Singlish, raising awareness of the importance of Standard English or simply increasing **appreciation** and sympathy for the Movement's goals).

[2] <u>Despite this, my concern about the ways in which Singlish is being understood and debated in the public sphere has continued to grow</u>. This is because there has been no significant change in the **premises** and parameters of the debate. Each time Singlish is discussed in public, the same arguments tend to be thrown up [1] and the same responses made. The result is that previously established views and attitudes (simplistically, either 'for' or 'against' Singlish because it is a 'good' or 'bad' thing) are further entrenched; there is no evidence of a closer meeting of minds, a better **appreciation** of different positions or a more nuanced understanding of the ideological assumptions involved.

1）非難・批判する、非難の対象として取り上げる

[3] <u>This book is born out of my concern with the ways in which the</u> <u>Singlish controversy has unfolded in public debates</u>. Though the impetus for the book is personal in nature, I have tried to provide an objective analysis of the controversy, looking at both sides of the debate. I should make clear, however, that the **points** I tried to convey to that senior civil servant all those years ago remain valid, and because of this, I am largely unsympathetic to those who would argue that Singlish is a problem, a linguistic menace that needs to be eliminated. This does not mean, however, that the arguments that have been proffered in favour [2] of Singlish are unproblematic. The arguments put forward [3] by the supporters as well as by the detractors of Singlish tend to be based on questionable assumptions.

[4] <u>In what follows, I show that viewing Singlish as a **liability** or</u> <u>an **asset** in fact sidesteps many of the important and complicated</u> <u>issues involved</u>. And because the issues involving the Singlish controversy are by no means unique to Singlish but are in fact relevant to broader concerns about language and identity in the context of rapid globalization [4], I am hopeful that the discussion in

---

2）アメリカ式の綴りでは "favor" となる。

3）意見や案などを出すこと

4）自分が何語の話者であるかということを自分のアイデンティティーの一部だと感じる人は多い（例えば自分は日本語を話すから日本人、と捉えるなど）が、言語がアイデンティティーにとって必須部分であるとは必ずしも言えないようである。移民3世や4世になると現地で使われている言語が母語となり、自分の出自文化で使われている言語を使えない場合も珍しくないが、それでも自分のアイデンティティーを祖先の出自文化に感じる場合もある（例えば日系アメリカ人が英語を母語としながらも自分は日系であると感じるなど）。

this book will be of interest to a fairly wide audience and not just those concerned with promoting or retarding the use of Singlish.

I. Understanding the Contents

下線を施した各パラグラフのトピック・センテンスを注意深く読み，それ以外は速読して，問1〜5に入る内容を，それぞれ選択肢a〜dの中から選びましょう。

問1　Singlish論争の現状について，ライオネル・ウィー氏の懸念が最も明確に述べられているのは……
　　a. 第1パラグラフ
　　b. 第2パラグラフ
　　c. 第3パラグラフ
　　d. 第4パラグラフ

問2　Singlish論争の中での，ライオネル・ウィー氏の立場が最も明確に表明されているのは……
　　a. 第1パラグラフ
　　b. 第2パラグラフ
　　c. 第3パラグラフ
　　d. 第4パラグラフ

問3　シンガポール政府の "Speak Good English Movement" というキャンペーンの主旨について述べられているのは……
　　a. 第1パラグラフ

　b. 第2パラグラフ

　c. 第3パラグラフ

　d. 第4パラグラフ

問4　このテキストは，*The Singlish Controversy: Language, Culture and Identity in a Globalizing World* と題された本の序文(Preface)です。この本全体の目的を説明しているのは……

　a. 第1パラグラフ

　b. 第2パラグラフ

　c. 第3パラグラフ

　d. 第4パラグラフ

問5　この本のサブタイトル（"Language, Culture and Identity in a Globalizing World"）の意味するところを最も明確に説明しているセンテンスを本文から抜き出してください。

II. The Opinions

プレゼンテーションの中の次の2つの部分を精読し，著者の主張をそれぞれ100字程度にまとめましょう。

Focus 1

Each time Singlish is discussed in public, the same arguments tend to be thrown up and the same responses made. The result is that previously established views and attitudes (simplistically, either 'for' or 'against' Singlish because it is a 'good' or 'bad' thing) are further entrenched; there is no evidence of a closer meeting of minds, a better appreciation of different positions or a more nuanced understanding of the ideological assumptions involved.

Focus 2

I should make clear, however, that the points I tried to convey to that senior civil servant all those years ago remain valid, and because of this, I am largely unsympathetic to those who would argue that Singlish is a problem, a linguistic menace that needs to be eliminated. This does not mean, however, that the arguments that have been proffered in favour of Singlish are unproblematic. The arguments put forward by the supporters as well as by the detractors of Singlish tend to be based on questionable assumptions.

III. Today's Vocabulary

以下の５つの単語について辞書を読み，さまざまな用例を理解した上で，本文中での用例を日本語に訳してみましょう。

appreciation, appreciative ← appreciate
・He appreciates various genres of music.
・She is good at appreciating the subtle changes in people's emotions.
・Your cooperation is much appreciated.

· This is a token of my appreciation.

· We were blessed with an appreciative audience.

I came to be more <u>appreciative</u> of the kinds of pressures that civil servants work under.

Running an official campaign such as the Speak Good English Movement meant having to show that some 'progress' was being made each year (such as reducing the rampant use of Singlish, raising awareness of the importance of standard English or simply increasing <u>appreciation</u> and sympathy for the Movement's goals).

There is no evidence of a closer meeting of minds, a better <u>appreciation</u> of different positions or a more nuanced understanding of the idealogical assumptions involved.

premise

· The premise must hold for the conclusion to be valid.

· There was a homeless person walking around the premises.

There has been no significant change in the <u>premises</u> and parameters of the debate.

point

· The Star of David has six points.

· There is an area called Long Point in the island.

· The leaf had many white points due to the plant disease.

· The raise was three point eight percent.

· He made a point of taking their daughter away from her.

· The point you made was crystal clear to me.

· The important point is to keep everything organized.

The points I tried to convey to that senior civil servant all those years ago remain valid.

liability

· The liability of this company is to be made good within a month.

· The lack of gender balance is a huge liability to the organization.

· The liability for the unfortunate incident lies with them, not us.

Viewing Singlish as a liability or an asset in fact sidesteps many of the important and complicated issues involved.

asset

· An unfaltering mind is a strong asset.

· Many unique cultural assets are displayed in the museum.

· The total assets held by the family amounts to 10 million dollars.

Viewing Singlish as a liability or an asset in fact sidesteps many of the important and complicated issues involved.

【発展的課題】

A．ライオネル・ウィー氏の著書のサブタイトルは「グローバル化する世界における言語・文化・アイデンティティー」となっています。「グローバル化する世界における言語・文化・アイデンティティー」という問題は，現在の日本にどのように関わっているでしょうか。

B．インターネット等で，シンガポールで使用されている言語の多様性について調べ，それを踏まえて，Singlish が用いられるように

なった背景，そして "Speak Good English Movement" というキャンペーンが行われた背景について考えなさい。

C．下の文章の組み立てや表現を可能な限り利用しながら，現在身のまわりで論争となっている問題について，どちらの陣営の主張にもそれぞれ問題があるという見解を表明する英文を書いてみましょう。

I am largely unsympathetic to those who would argue that Singlish is a problem, a linguistic menace that needs to be eliminated. This does not mean, however, that the arguments that have been proffered in favour of Singlish are unproblematic. The arguments put forward by the supporters as well as by the detractors of Singlish tend to be based on questionable assumptions.

【コラム】　　■ ■　**グローバル・キャンパス**　■ ■

　この章で紹介されている激論は、2000年代初めのシンガポール国立大学の会議室で交わされたとのことですが、この時期には世界中の大学の会議室が過熱状態にあったようで、私自身の体験もその例に漏れません。世界中の大学で、喧々諤々の議論が交わされ、ありとあらゆる改革が試みられた時代でした。その中で日本の大学のキャンパスも様変わりしたことを生々しく思い出します。

　この授業でインタビューした方々の多くとそしてクリスティー先生自身が、つくば市の大学や研究機関にやってきて、日本社会のメンバーに加わったのもほぼその時期にあたります。いわゆる「留学生30万人計画」が策定された2008年という年は、そのような変化が起こり始めた年として目安になります。なぜそのような変化が起こったのでしょうか?

　医学においては、知識の倍増に要する時間が、1950年には50年を要し、それが1980年には7年になり、そして2020年には73日にまで短縮されるという試算がなされたことがあります。大学生が入学してから卒業するまでの4年間に、ひとつの学問分野の知識量が倍増してしまうことになります。このような加速が起これば、大学がかつてのままでいられるはずもありません。また国境を越えた教育と研究を展開しなければ、このようなハイスピードのレースに勝ち残れないと多くの人が考えるようになったのも当然です。

　大学と研究機関が集中した研究学園都市であるつくば市では、それゆえにグローバル化が急速に展開しました。ふと気がつくと、大学の喫茶室で隣の席から外国語が聞こえてきてもそれが普通になり、学内にハラールの学食が誕生し、私の所属していた筑波大学の人文社会科学研究科では留学生が半数を越えていました。

　そのような中で、それまでには考えられなかったような授業ができるようになりました。例えば日本人と留学生がちょうど同数の教室で、日本社会のグロー

バル化の課題について英語のみによるディスカッションを1学期間展開した授業など、鮮烈な記憶として残っています。私は正直なところ日本の大学生にこれほどの英語ディベート能力があるとは思ってもみませんでした。大学院生数名を毎年カリフォルニア大学バークレー校に引率して、丸1週間アメリカの大学の教育方法を視察し、バークレーの教員と討議し、共同で報告書を作成するプロジェクトなど、私自身の教育観を大きく変える体験になりました。

　日本の大学教育の公用語を英語に切り替えれば、世界中から優れた学生と研究者を言葉の障壁なしに迎え入れることができるようになり、とくに理系の研究水準が飛躍的に向上することは目に見えています。しかしその場合、小学校から大学院まで一貫して母語による教育を提供している日本の教育のユニークな特性は、日本語固有の発想とともに失われることになるかもしれません。そのことをパトリシア・ライアンの TED Talks は教えてくれます。

　この時期に起こった目まぐるしい変化の、すべてがよかったとは思いません。しかし何がよい改革で何が必ずしもそうではなかったかを判断するのは、難しいことです。例えば5年後にその成果を判定するのと、50年後にその成果を判定するのとでは、当然違う結論が出るでしょう。

　たくさんの答えのない問いと向き合った大学の会議室が、しばしば炎上寸前になったのも無理はありません。

（宮本陽一郎）

Chapter 12 Conversation with Herb Fondevilla (1)

Herb L. Fondevilla moved to Japan from the Philippines in 2006 to pursue graduate studies and received a PhD in Art Studies from the University of Tsukuba. She is currently a Visiting Researcher at the Institute of Island Studies at Meiji University and teaches part-time at Mejiro University and Yokohama National University. Her research interests include Japanese visual culture and its impact and interpretation outside of Japan, community-based art projects and initiatives, and the benefits of the arts on health and wellbeing.

K: Thank you so much for coming and talking with us today, Herb.

H: Thank you for having me.

K: Would you be able to just introduce yourself to our listeners, and tell us a bit about you and what you do? Thank you.

H: Okay, so my name is Herb Fondevilla. I'm currently a visiting researcher at Meiji University. So my research **concerns** art, contemporary art, and arts and health, which is not very common. And I also do some research on arts and its benefits in persons living with dementia.

K: Wow, that's really cool. Now, where are you from originally?

H: I'm originally from the Philippines. I was born and raised in Quezon City[1].

K: Cool. Philippines is beautiful.

H: Thank you.

K: How long have you been living in Japan?

H: It's funny you ask that. Because, as I mentioned earlier, I came to Japan thinking I would stay for two years, and now it has been 15 whopping years.

K: It's amazing how time flies.

H: Indeed. I never thought I'd stay this long here in Japan, but you know here we are, and here I am. Still here.

K: It happens to all of us, it seems. What brought you to Japan and what made you stay?

---

1) フィリピンの大マニラ首都圏を構成する都市のひとつ。首都マニラの北東に隣接する。1948年から1976年にかけて首都が置かれた。

H: I came to Japan on a scholarship. I received a scholarship from All Nippon Airways.

K: Hah! I did not know that. Okay.

H: So most people come to Japan on Japanese government scholarships. I came on an All Nippon Airways scholarship. And I came here because I was very interested—I still am, actually—in Japanese pop culture and how it's influencing our lives in a contemporary culture. And I came here to study that. And I thought I was just going to do my master's for three years, and then go back to the Philippines and work in advertising. But things happened. And 15 years on I'm still here.

K: Can you tell me . . . What languages do you speak? And where and when do you use them?

H: Yeah, that's very interesting. So I was born in the Philippines and we speak two languages. We have two national languages, Filipino and English [2]. We use them both in education, in law, in media, almost everywhere. When I was growing up, I remember we had this school rule where you have to pay one peso for every Filipino word that you speak. They were pretty strict about it. And I don't think it's very common.

K: And so it was to **discourage** you from using your national language.

---

2) ここでは公用語の意味で national language という表現を使っているが、通常は国語を national language、公用語を official language と表現することが多い。Herb はこの2語を区別しないで使っている。

H: Yeah, one of the national languages. Because, when I was growing up, I've also lived with my grandmother, and she spoke a dialect which is called Romblomanon[3]. Growing up, I had to master Filipino, English, and had to learn how to understand Romblomanon. And my mom is half Chinese, so she also spoke to me sometimes in Chinese, though I never picked up Chinese. So growing up, I was surrounded by four languages. But I think this is very usual for many Filipino families, because, Filipino and English, you just really need to study them. But many families also have roots in other places, other provinces, other islands. They also use another dialect. So many kids in the Philippines grew up with at least three.

K: That is amazing. Wow. Do you think now there is sort of a hierarchy or a prioritization of English over Filipino?

H: This's interesting. When I was growing up, . . . now I have to reveal my age.

K: Still younger than me.

H: I know. But during the 80s, English was very much in use. And I think in 1987 the country ratified the new constitution, which said that now our official languages are Filipino and English. But in the 90s, there was a movement to actually use more Filipino. I think that came from the media when they started dubbing a lot of shows in Filipino. We used to get a lot

---

3）ロンブロン島をはじめとするフィリピンの地方で話されている言語。2015年の時点で 94,000 人の話者がいるとされる。〈https://en.wikipedia.org/wiki/Romblomanon_language〉

of movies, cartoons, from the United States. Everything was dubbed in English. So growing up, I didn't know where these shows came from. I knew they were American. Even anime. I thought anime was from the US, because everything was in English. TV commercials were in English, The books that I read, the newspapers, were all in English. But in the 90s, there was a new movement to encourage people to use more Filipino. So I think the current generation, those kids who were born in the late 90s to early 2000s, I think they grew up hearing more Filipino in the media than when I was a kid in the 80s. So there has been, I think, a shift in the way that we use language now.

I. Understanding the Contents

インタビューを速読して，問1～5に入る内容を，それぞれ選択肢a～dの中から選びましょう。

問1　ハーブさんが日本にくるきっかけとなったのは……
　a. 日本政府の奨学金を得たこと
　b. フィリピン政府の奨学金を得たこと
　c. 民間企業の奨学金を得たこと
　d. 日本の広告会社への就職

問2　ハーブさんの日本滞在歴は……
　a. 2年

　b. 5 年

　c. 10 年

　d. 15 年以上

問 3　フィリピンの学校で用いられる言語は……

　a. スペイン語のみ

　b. フィリピン語のみ

　c. 英語とフィリピン語

　d. ロンブロマノン語とタガログ語

問 4　1990 年代にフィリピンでは……

　a. アメリカ映画の影響で英語の使用が日常的になった。

　b. フィリピン語の使用がはばかられる傾向が顕著になった。

　c. フィリピン語の使用が推奨されるようになった。

　d. 中国語も実質的な公用語になった。

問 5　ハーブさんに比べて現在のフィリピンの子どもたちは……

　a. メディアを通じて英語に接する機会が多い。

　b. メディアを通じてフィリピン語に接する機会が多い。

　c. メディアを通じてスペイン語に接する機会が多い。

　d. メディアを通じて多様な方言に接する機会が多い。

II. The Opinions

インタビューの中の次の３つの部分を精読し，ハーブさんの主張をそれ
ぞれ 100 字程度にまとめましょう。

Focus 1

H: Historically speaking, we have Tagalog. But the Philippines has a
lot of regional dialects[4] . And the Tagalog being the language of
the northern provinces, people from other provinces don't think
it's fair that the Philippines chose Tagalog as the base language
of the national language. So **technically** speaking, the national
language is Filipino. But Filipino is based on Tagalog, which is a
dialect.

K: Okay. I didn't know that. So Filipino and Tagalog are not the same
thing.

H: No. So when you say Filipino, it's Tagalog with Spanish words in
it, some English words in it, it's a mixed language. You can say
it's like Creole[5] . But not many Filipinos know this technicality.
So when people ask me, "What is the national language of the

4）外務省のウェブサイトには「80 前後の言語がある」と記されている〈https://
www.mofa.go.jp/mofaj/area/philippines/data.html〉が、フィリピン政府観光省
のウェブサイトには「80 以上の民族グループには、100 以上の言語、500 以上の
方言があります。主な言語グループは、タガログ（マニラ周辺）、セブアノ（ビサ
ヤ地方）、イロカノ（北部ルソン）、ビコール（南部ルソン）、ワライ、パンガシナ
ン、マラナオなど［後略］」と記されている〈https://philippinetravel.jp/about/
basic/〉。https://www.muturzikin.com/cartesasiesudest/5.htm を参照するとこの
インタビューで言及される言語が話されている地域が大体わかる。
5）母語話者を持つ混成言語

Philippines?" I always say, "It's Filipino," because that's what's written in our constitution.

K: If somebody said, "What is the language of the Philippines?" I would have said, "Tagalog," and it's not.

H: No, it's not. It's Filipino . . .

K: New information!

H: . . . with an F. It used to be spelled with a P and then they changed it to F.

K: Why?

H: To recognize our background, you know, as having had Spanish, and American, and, of course, a local language thrown in. To emphasize that this is a mixed culture, a mixed language. But however, other people would say, it's not fair that the country based the national language on Tagalog, wherein there are languages such as Cebuano or Hiligaynon [6]. And they don't think it's fair. If you go to the Philippines you may notice that some Filipinos don't even want to speak Tagalog. They don't **accept** it.

Focus 2

K: Do you consider yourself a native English speaker?

H: I consider myself as a bilingual, native English speaker. It's funny how people would define what is a native English speaker. Because there are many native English speakers, but they all speak in different accents. So a lot of Filipinos have been studying, have been learning, have been hearing English, from the moment

---

6）どちらもフィリピン中部で話されている言語。

they were born. But they don't necessarily speak it, because it makes you sound like a snob if you just speak to people in English. Like, "Why are you speaking in plain and straight English to people when it's not supposed to be just your only language? You're supposed to have at least two."

K: Do you feel that you are **perceived** as a native English speaker?

H: No, I don't think so. And I think there's a hierarchy of how people look at or define what native speakers are. And I think they define them from where they are from, or their citizenship, mostly their passports. So, I would say that it's really undefined. I have met so many people from India, from Pakistan, and they speak really good English. And I think they also consider themselves as native English speakers. We all just speak in different accents. And you can't **fault** us, because of globalization. I mean, if the Americans, or if the British didn't want English to spread this far and wide, then they shouldn't have crossed the seas and left us alone, right? But they did, and so this happened.

Focus 3

H: I think here in Japan, especially when they think of what a native English speaker is, I think they would consider first what this person looks like. Is this person the typical white person: blue eyes, blond hair. And what country is that person from. Are they from US, Canada, UK, Australia, and then it goes on and on. But the Philippines is like at the bottom of the ladder. And I think there are reasons for that, other than the Japanese idea of what a native English speaker looks like. I think it's economics.

III. Today's Vocabulary

以下の6つの単語について辞書を読み，さまざまな用例を理解した上で，本文中での用例を日本語に訳してみましょう。

concern

・Protecting the environment concerns us all.

・His major is concerned with literature.

・She was concerned about her sister's health.

・I have a concern about how to carry out the plan.

My research <u>concerns</u> art.

discourage

・He was quite discouraged by her decision.

・The recession discouraged people from buying new products.

・I strongly discourage you from drinking.

And so it was to <u>discourage</u> you from using your national language.

technically

・This piece is technically very challenging to play.

・Technically, they are not siblings.

・Technically, this statement is contradictory to the doctrine.

So <u>technically</u> speaking, the national language is Filipino.

accept

· She accepted his apologies.

· Please accept this small token of my appreciation.

· He was accepted to ten different universities.

· You must learn to accept your own limitations.

· The testimony was accepted as describing what really happened.

They don't <u>accept</u> it.

perceive

· I perceive an unusual animal in the distance.

· He perceived her to be a gentle person.

· She perceived the change in altitude by the discomfort in her eardrum.

Do you feel that you are <u>perceived</u> as a native English speaker?

fault

· Don't try to find faults with your neighbor.

· It's not your fault that things turned out the way it did.

· There was a fault in his plan.

· She could not fault him for chipping her favorite plate.

And you can't <u>fault</u> us, because of globalization.

発展的課題

A．ハーブさんが解説してくれたフィリピンにおけるさまざまな言語
　の共存や混交を踏まえながら、日本における標準語、方言、外来
　語の関係について論じてください。

B．ハーブさんの指摘を踏まえつつ、みなさん自身が「ネイティヴ・
　スピーカー」「英語母語話者」という概念をどのように捉えていた
　のか考えてみましょう。

C．B.について，ハーブさんの指摘について、補足あるいは反論があ
　れば、それを英語で述べてください。

【コラム】　　　■■　　清次の幻影　　■■

　『新・悪名』（1962 年）という映画は、第二次世界大戦後の占領下日本とそ
の文化的混乱を活写した、隠れた名作だと思っています。今東光の小説『悪名』
から派生した、「悪名」シリーズの映画の第三作にあたります。

　この映画で、主役の朝吉親分（勝新太郎）は、戦前に一の子分だった「モー
トルの貞」の生き写しの弟と、米軍基地のフェンスの前で偶然出会うことに。「モー
トルの貞」も弟の清次も、田宮二郎が演じているので、確かに生き写しです。

　顔がそっくりとは言え、清次は、ひとかどの（?）やくざだった「モートルの貞」
とは似ても似つかないチンピラです。米軍基地に出入りして、闇物資を売買し、
売春を取りしきりと、やりたい放題です。真っ赤なセーターに黒の革ジャンにG
パンにハンティングという支離滅裂な出立ちで、ジープに乗って颯爽と登場し、
英語混じりの関西弁あるいは関西弁混じりの英語で、朝吉親分を煙にまきます。
「けったくそわるい……英語ばかり使いよって」と朝吉親分は吐き捨てます。「英
語がぺらぺら」という言い方は、すっかり時代遅れになったのかもしれませんが、
その「ぺらぺら」という表現につきまとう軽薄さのイメージを、この映画の田宮
二郎ほど見事に演じきった例は稀です。

　ハーブさんのインタビューの中では、フィリピンにおいて英語で話すことが忌
避されたり逆にトレンド化したりという紆余曲折が興味深く語られていましたが、
それが現在のフィリピンの文化の固有性を生んだということができます。

　同様に「ぺらぺら」であることが「けったくそわるい」と感じる心は、日本の
戦後体験の中で醸成された固有の文化でしょう。そのような意味での「英語苦
手意識」を私は非難したくはありません。それがあったからこそ現在の日本文
化があるのだと思います。

　しかし、現在の日本人が英語によるコミュニケーションの必要を感じるのであ
れば、どこかでしかるべきかたちで清次の幻影とお別れしなければならないの
かもしれません。

　　　　　　　　　　　　　　　　　　　　　　　　　　　　（宮本陽一郎）

Chapter 13

Conversation with Herb Fondevilla (2)

Herb L. Fondevilla's research enables her to collaborate with scholars and researchers around the world, and offers her a unique insight into the ways in which Japanese popular culture and contemporary society are perceived by people outside of Japan. In addition to this, as a non-Japanese Japanese Studies expert, she is in an unusual position to observe Japanese society as both an insider and an outsider. Herb aspires to write a book someday.

K: What advantages and disadvantages have you personally experienced with your unique linguistic background?

H: Advantages would be, in Japan, one of the better-paid jobs for foreigners is teaching English. And ever since I came to Japan, I came here as a student, and I get 2,000 yen per hour for teaching English. If you compare that to working at a convenience store, that's 980 yen per hour, and that's a lot of money. It's a big difference. The disadvantage is that people still judge you from where you come from, and from what you look like, when it comes to jobs. And it's interesting. I'm not sure if people have discussed this, but in Japan, and if you're a foreigner, and the better you are at speaking Japanese, in a way you get more **integrated** into the culture, and the more pressure is put on you. And a lot of people, like, even for me . . . I noticed that, that the more you appear to not understand Japanese, in a way the better you are treated, and I think it's sometimes really strange.

K: What's behind that?   Because I agree with you.

H: Even I am still like . . . I am, you know, because for me sometimes, like . . . they call it the *gaijin* card, right? If you want to get out of trouble . . .

K: Play the *gaijin* card.

H: . . . play the *gaijin* card, because people treat you better if they think you are stupid than if you try to **assimilate**. And you try very hard to speak Japanese, and then they treat you worse because you speak Japanese and because you understand Japanese culture. But at the same time, they have to understand, you are doing this to the best of your abilities, but you are still not Japanese, and you still need help; "But I am trying my best, please help me." But if you're like, "I don't care about your culture," I'm just going to speak whatever language I can use, and you, just do what you can.[1] I don't understand it either.

K: Yeah, it is. It's so interesting that there seems to be kind of these different levels of fluency that we reach when we've stayed here and tried to **invest** in learning. In the beginning if you do a couple of *aisatsu* . . .

H: It makes me afraid, you know.

K: And if your *hashi* are *jozu*,

H: Yeah, I know, I was like, what . . . it's . . . chopsticks.

K: Yeah, and at that point you get so much praise for just such basic kind of Japanese. But then, the more advanced you get, there's a turn[2].

H: Yes. This is like, you reach this level and then suddenly they don't like you anymore, and it's like, "What?!"

K: Or at least you're no longer going to get the assistance, because now you're on your own.

H: I know, and it's really strange to me, because I thought that people would treat you better, because they know that you

1）明言されていないが、「そうすればかえって丁重に扱ってもらえる」という趣旨の意図である。
2）方向転換

understand Japanese already.

K: And that you're **investing** in trying to learn. Yeah.

H: But at the same time, there are so many things in Japan that still don't make sense to me even after 15 years. One of them is apartments. So looking for an apartment, my experience was that . . . when I moved to Yokohama, I had to go to a real estate agency[3] and asked them if I could rent this apartment. The first thing the real estate agent did was to call the owner and tell them that a foreigner wants to rent an apartment. And most of them, I would say 90%, said no [4]. And then, I would tell them, "Tell the owner that I speak Japanese," and then your odds go up. Maybe, maybe they will let you rent the apartment because you speak Japanese.

K: Yeah, show some responsibility.

H: And I hear that it's because foreigners don't know how to take out the trash, they are noisy. They have parties, and stuff like that. But I think these are just, again, presumptions. Not all foreigners like to party and don't care about taking out the trash. Because, you know, I have been here for 15 years. I am **invested** in this country, and I do know how to take out the trash properly, and I don't have parties all the time in my house.

K: And locals *may*, you know, it could be an **issue** that parties

---

3）不動産業者

4）残念ながら 2021 年現在でも珍しいことではない。

〈https://resources.realestate.co.jp/ja/living/top-5-reasons-rental-applications-are-rejected-by-landlords-in-japan-jp/〉

might be by local people.

H: And I think it's also because of the media. Whenever foreigners do something bad, it's all over the news.

I. Understanding the Contents

インタビューを速読して，問1〜5に入る内容を，それぞれ選択肢a〜dの中から選びましょう。

問1　ハーブさんのように，英語が話せる外国人が日本で暮らす利点は……
　　a. 外資系の会社に就職できること
　　b. 英語教員として高い収入が得られること
　　c. 通訳としての仕事がいつでも得られること
　　d. 日本の広告会社への就職

問2　日本では，初歩的な日本語しか話せない外国人は……
　　a. 日本社会の中に入れてもらえない。
　　b. 寛容に扱われる。
　　c. 常に奇異の目で見られる。
　　d. 信用されない。

問3　"play the *gaijin* card" とはどのような意味であると推測されますか？
　　a. 在留カードを申請する。
　　b. 在留カードをちらつかせる。
　　c. 外国人であることを切り札にする。
　　d. 外国人であることを楽しむ。

問4　日本では，外国人がある程度以上に日本語を習得すると……

　　a. ようやく日本社会の一員として認められる。

　　b. かえって冷たく扱われる。

　　c. 非常に寛容な扱いを受けられるようになる。

　　d. 高い給与が保証される。

問5　外国人が日本でアパートを借りるのが難しい理由として，インタビューの中で挙げられて<u>いない</u>ものは，次のどれですか？

　　a. 犯罪との結びつきが疑われる。

　　b. パーティーをやって騒ぐというイメージがある。

　　c. ゴミの出し方のルールを守らないと思われている。

　　d. 法律上の制約がある。

II. The Opinions

インタビューの中の次の3つの部分を精読し，ハーブさんの主張をそれぞれ100字程度にまとめましょう。

Focus 1

K: Maybe it builds a **case** for having a global language. If we all share one language, would that put everybody on the same playing field[5]?

H: I think so. At the same time, there are **issues** around it, English as a global language, because it does speak of colonization.

K: That's really problematic, isn't it?　Yeah.

5）競技場。put ○○ on the same playing field はいわば「同じ土俵に乗せる」と同じこと。

H: The hegemony. The hegemony of Western cultures.

Focus 2

K: Do you think it's a good idea to have English as a common language worldwide?　Why or why not?

H: I think it's a very loaded question[6]. Personally, because I already speak English, it's good for me. It's to my advantage to have English as a global language. I know how hard it is to learn, to master another language. Having studied Japanese and having lived in Japan all these years, Japanese is not an easy language to master. And even Japanese people themselves are still . . . it takes an entire lifetime to master their own language. I always tell my students, the English alphabet only has twenty-six letters. So much easier. It's easier to look things up in the dictionary, it's only twenty-six letters. But at the same time, if you go deeper into the **issues**, this is the history of colonization. The hegemony of Western cultures. At the same time, at this stage in history, at this moment in history, how are we going to choose? What side are you on?　Shall we speak English?　Should we speak Chinese? Technically, there are more Chinese speakers in the world[7].

---

6) 複雑な質問、意味深長な質問

7) 文部科学省のウェブサイトでは、2005 年のデータとして、中国語母語話者数が 885,000,000、英語の母語話者数が 400,000,000、とされている。〈https://www.mext. go.jp/b_menu/shingi/chukyo/chukyo3/004/siryo/attach/1379956.htm〉

Focus 3

K: I've always thought we should go with Esperanto[8] and have this artificially created language that has no cultural backup.

H: But that would mean upending all the research that has been done in the past and all of the documents and all of the academic learning. Do we translate them all to Esperanto?

K: Good question. Yeah, the Internet seems to have fixed it. Now that it is on the Internet and everybody is connected that way, it's almost like English has become the de facto[9] language.

III. Today's Vocabulary

以下の5つの単語について辞書を読み，さまざまな用例を理解した上で，本文中での用例を日本語に訳してみましょう。

integrate

・He integrated what he learned to write a comprehensive book.

・The orientation sessions help new students integrate into university life.

・You must integrate your skills with your knowledge.

・People from various backgrounds are integrated in the community.

The better you are at speaking Japanese, in a way you get more integrated into the culture.

8）ポーランド人の眼科医であり言語学者でもあったザメンホフによって作り出された人造国際語。

9）事実上、実際には

invest

· I invested my savings in real estate.

· He invests a lot of time and money in going to concerts.

· The mascot invests the school with an air of friendliness.

· The board is invested with the power to make the final decision.

· She invested in a gorgeous dress.

We've stayed here and tried to <u>invest</u> in learning.

You're <u>investing</u> in trying to learn.

I am <u>invested</u> in this country.

case

· A similar case was reported in the other paper.

· If that is the case, there is nothing we can do about it.

· The case is currently under investigation.

· They made a good case for equal opportunity between men and women.

· There were five heart attack cases this week.

· He filed a case for divorce.

· "My" is the possessive case for "I".

Maybe it builds a <u>case</u> for having a global language.

issue

· New commemorative stamps were issued on January 1st.

· The newest issue of the magazine has arrived in stores.

· This island has been a cause of diplomatic issues for a long time.

· The quarrel between the brothers was brought to issue by their father.

At the same time, there are <u>issues</u> around it, English as a global language.

If you go deeper into the <u>issues</u>, this is the history of colonization.

assimilate

・She assimilated the memories of her overseas trips in the drawing.

・He assimilated his behaviour to those around him.

・The newcomers were assimilated into the club very quickly.

People treat you better if they think you are stupid than if you try to <u>assimilate</u>.

[発展的課題]

Ａ．ハーブさんは，インタビューの中で，外国人がアパートを借りる
　　際の困難について語っていました。この問題を解決するためには
　　どうしたらよいでしょう。

Ｂ．日本人の「ガイジン」に対する接し方について，ハーブさんはイ
　　ンタビューの中で語っていました。なぜ日本人はそのような接し
　　方をするのか，英語で説明してください。

Ｃ．ハーブさんのインタビュー，およびこれまでに取り上げたさまざ
　　まなインタビューを踏まえつつ，"Do you think it's a good idea
　　to have English as a common language worldwide? Why or
　　why not?" という問いに対するあなた自身の答えを英語で述べて
　　ください。

【コラム】　　■■　**複数言語の使い分け**　■■

　複数の言語が使える人は、自分が使える言語を何らかの形で使い分けること
が多いですが、使い分けのパターンの最も一般的なものとして「人によって使い
分ける」というものと、「場面によって使い分ける」というものがあります。

　複数の養育者（例えば父親と母親）が異なる言語で子育てをした場合に、子
どもはそれぞれの養育者が自分に話しかける言語を区別し、それぞれの言語で
応えようとする時期があります。これは「人によって使い分ける」パターンの最も
典型的な例ですが、特定の言語を特定の人と結びつけて考えているため、養育
者が通常とは別の言語を使うと怒りさえすることもあるようです。一方、家庭内
で使っている言語と社会で使われている言語が異なっているときに、同じ相手
に対して状況次第で複数の言語を使う場合は、「場面によって使い分ける」典型
例です。例えば家の中ではきょうだい同士でそれぞれの母語で話していても一
歩家を出ると同じきょうだいに対して学校で使われている言語で話す、というよ
うな形があり得ます。

　これらの2つのパターンでは、ある程度まとまった形で片方の言語を使うこと
がイメージされます（例えば特定の相手には1つの言語を使い続けたり、家を出
てから再び家に帰るまでは1つの言語を使い続けるなど）が、相手が自分と同
じ複数言語を使える場合に限って、もっと頻繁に言語を使い分けることがあり
ます。例えばカナダの病院で英仏両言語に堪能な看護師2人が英語話者の患
者に対応している時に、基本的には英語でやり取りしている中で、患者に聞か
せたくない内容についてお互いに確認する時にフランス語でやり取りする、とい
う例では、その確認のための短いやり取りのところのみ言語を使い分けるという
ことになります。さらに、この2人の看護師が当人同士だけでやり取りをする時
に、一文の中に英語の単語とフランス語の単語を混ぜて話すことなどもあり得ま
す。

　複数の言語が使えるといっても、それらの言語を完全に同レベルで同等に使えるということは珍しく、言語間に得意・不得意があることの方が普通です。どの程度得意であればその言語を「使える」と言えるのかについての決まりはありません。英語が不得意な気がしてもなるべく積極的に使っていき、使うことで徐々に得意になっていくことを目指したいものです。

（大橋理枝）

Part Ⅴ

Global Citizenship

Chapters 14 ～ 15
（扉）

Chapter 14 Kuei Yai, "Global citizen"

▲ 地球温暖化に抗議する子どもたちの「グローバル・ストライキ」(2019年3月)

(写真提供：ユニフォトプレス)

Kuei Yai's TED talk was recorded at a TEDxYouth event in Nairobi, Kenya, in 2017. At that time, Ms. Yai was in the 12th grade at Brookhouse School, in Nairobi, and her talk focused on the importance of global citizenship. Brookhouse School has been organizing an independent TEDxYouth conference in November each year since 2013, and the theme of Kuei's year was 'Shaping the Future'.

[1] <u>What is the first thing that comes to mind</u>[1] <u>when you're</u> <u>asked "what do we all have in common?"</u> We're humans? We all have a common ancestry? Or perhaps the fact that we all share one home—earth. This means that we are responsible for it and whatever happens. Therefore, what is the correct concept in which this responsibility is **recognized**?

[2] <u>Ladies and gentlemen, let me introduce you to global</u> <u>citizenship.</u> Global citizenship is defined as a way of living that **recognizes** that our world is increasing web of connections and interdependencies, one in which our decisions and actions may have repercussions on the community.

[3] <u>I consider myself as a global citizen, as someone who</u> <u>identifies with being part of an emerging community and whose</u> <u>actions contribute to the community's values.</u> Even so, I am not abandoning my identity such as my allegiance to my country South Sudan[2] or my ethnicity and my beliefs. These traditional

---

1 ）心に浮かぶ

2 ）南スーダン共和国。日本の約 1.7 倍に当たる 64 万 km² の国土に 1,258 万人（2017 年）の人口を擁す。首都はジュバ。多民族国家であり、英語が公用語とされている。国内ではその他にもアラビア語も使われており、その他部族語も多数話されている。

〈https://www.mofa.go.jp/mofaj/area/s_sudan/data. html#section1〉

identities give meaning to my life and help shape who I am. However, as a result of living in a globalized world, I understand that I have an added layer of responsibility. We are responsible for being members of a worldwide community of people who share the same global identity that we have.

[4] Climate change—climate change is one of the major challenges of our time and adds considerable stress to both our societies and the environment. It is **due** to our selfish reasons that food production is affected and as we speak, Kenya faces food shortages **due** to recurring droughts. Did you know that a report by the UN states that one in nine people do not get enough food to be healthy and lead an active life? In addition, around 29,000 children under the age of five die every day around the world[3]. This is **due** to preventable causes like poverty and malnutrition and etc., but rarely makes headline news. Sadly, too often we focus on what divides us but shouldn't we unite ourselves? Historically, people have always formed communities based on shared identity. Shouldn't our leaders unite us rather than use divisive rhetoric[4]?

---

3) UNICEF の資料によれば、2019 年の 5 歳未満児童の年間死亡者数は 5,189,000 と推定されており、これは日割り計算すると 14,000 強になる。〈https://data.unicef. org/topic/child-survival/under-five-mortality/〉

4)「美辞麗句」や「修辞」と訳されることも多いが、ここでは話す際の言葉の選び方を指している。

[5] I appeal to all of you sitting here to **embrace** the idea of a global identity. The world faces global challenges which require global solutions. This calls for [5] far-reaching changes in how we think and act. And I believe that global citizenship is the key to shaping our future because it helps us create a sense of **belonging** to a common humanity, creating a fairer world and hence helping learners to feel **obligated** and responsible to be active global citizens.

[6] The youth can learn to be active global citizens through global citizenship education. This is a form of **civic** learning that **involves** students' active participation in projects that are just global issues of an environmental, political, social, or economic nature. It educates and prepares people for their role in the modern world which begins with an exploration and appreciation of different cultures, languages, and economies. For example at Brookhouse [6], global citizenship is achieved through diverse engagement such as internationalism and learning foreign languages, to name a couple. These activities help us to become more open-minded

---

5）要する、必要とする

6）ケニアのナイロビに 1981 年に創立された共学の私立学校。通学生と寮生を受け入れており、幼稚園から高校まである。イギリス式の教育理念に基づいた教育を行っており、国際的な私立学校連盟である Round Square 〈https://www.roundsquare.org/〉や G-30 〈http://www.g30schools.org/〉のメンバーでもある。
Round Square については玉川学園の説明が詳しい。〈https://www.tamagawa.jp/introduction/enkaku/history/detail_14659.html〉

and to bridge cultural gaps which make us better global citizens.

[7] Imagine living in a world without worrying about global chill [7]. Imagine living in a world without war or poverty. <u>Action on our issues is cheaper than inaction</u>. If we all participate in the search for solutions to our global issues as active global citizens, then we'd live sustainably in a more equitable world. After all, actions do speak louder than words [8]. Therefore, I urge you all to be great global citizens. If we don't solve our issues, if we don't save our planet, and if our words are meaningless, then what future will we have to shape? In the words of Wangari Maathai [9], it is the little things that citizens do—that's what will make the difference. Wouldn't you want to be remembered because of the small difference you made in this world?

Thank you.

7）経済的な冷え込み

8）Actions speak louder than words「行いは言葉より雄弁である」という諺が元。do は強調。

9）ワンガリ・マータイ（1940-2011）。アメリカで高等教育を受けた後、ケニアのナイロビ大学で獣医学の博士号を取得。植林活動を熱心に行い、グリーンベルト運動に繋げた。後に政界入りし、2002 年にケニアの国会議員に初当選。2004 年にノーベル平和賞受賞。日本語の「もったいない」を世界に広め、Mottainai 運動を始めた人でもある。〈https://www.nobelprize.org/prizes/peace/2004/maathai/biographical/〉〈http://www.mottainai.info/jp/about/〉

I. Understanding the Contents

下線を施した各パラグラフのトピック・センテンスを注意深く読み，それ以外は速読して，問1～5に入る内容を，それぞれ選択肢 a～d の中から選びましょう。

問1　クェイ・ヤイさんが冒頭で掲げた "what do we all have in common?" という問いに対する答えは……
　　a. our ancestry
　　b. our citizenship
　　c. our language
　　d. our environment

問2　"Global citizenship" という言葉を定義しているのは……
　　a. 第2パラグラフ
　　b. 第3パラグラフ
　　c. 第5パラグラフ
　　d. 第6パラグラフ

問3　"Global citizenship" という概念の必要性を生み出した背景として，プレゼンテーションの中では言及されていないものは……
　　a. 食糧危機
　　b. 気候変動
　　c. 金融危機
　　d. 貧困問題

問4　"Global citizenship education" で扱うべき内容として，プレゼンテーションの中では言及されていないものは……

a. 異文化理解
b. 環境論
c. 国際法規
d. 外国語教育

問5　"Global citizenship" に関して，クェイ・ヤイさんが最も大切だと考えることは……
a. 行動を起こすこと
b. お互いを理解し合うこと
c. 経済的な平等を確立すること
d. 異文化に対して寛容になること

II. The Opinions

プレゼンテーションの中の次の2つの部分を精読し，著者の論点をそれぞれ100字程度にまとめましょう。

Focus 1

I consider myself as a global citizen, as someone who identifies with being part of an emerging community and whose actions contribute to the community's values. Even so, I am not abandoning my identity such as my allegiance to my country South Sudan or my ethnicity and my beliefs. These traditional identities give meaning to my life and help shape who I am. However, as a result of living in a globalized world, I understand that I have an added layer of responsibility. We are responsible for being members of a worldwide community of people who share the same global identity that we have.

Focus 2

Imagine living in a world without worrying about global chill. Imagine living in a world without war or poverty. Action on our issues is cheaper than inaction. If we all participate in the search for solutions to our global issues as active global citizens, then we'd live sustainably in a more equitable world. After all, actions do speak louder than words. Therefore, I urge you all to be great global citizens. If we don't solve our issues, if we don't save our planet, and if our words are meaningless, then what future will we have to shape? In the words of Wangari Maathai, it is the little things that citizens do—that's what will make the difference. Wouldn't you want to be remembered because of the small difference you made in this world?

III. Today's Vocabulary

以下の7つの単語について辞書を読み，さまざまな用例を理解した上で，本文中での用例を日本語に訳してみましょう。

recognize

What is the correct concept in which this responsibility is <u>recognized</u>? Global citizenship is defined as a way of living that <u>recognizes</u> that our world is increasing web of connections and interdependencies. Even I couldn't recognize my dad's name. (Chapter 1)

due

· The due date is this coming Friday.

· An apology is due to him.

· It is the prisoners' rights to receive due treatment.

· The train is due to arrive in 10 minutes.

· The vegetable prices are rising due to bad weather.

It is <u>due</u> to our selfish reasons that food production is affected and as we speak, Kenya faces food shortages <u>due</u> to recurring droughts.

This is <u>due</u> to preventable causes like poverty and malnutrition.

embrace

· His daughter stopped crying when he embraced her.

· They embrace the idea that eating meat is cruel to animals.

· You must learn to embrace bad luck.

· The group embraces people from different backgrounds.

· She embraces Hinduism.

I appeal to all of you sitting here to <u>embrace</u> the idea of a global identity.

belonging, obligate → obligation, oblige

· Take your personal belongings with you.

· People often wish for a feeling of belonging to somewhere.

· I am obligated to fulfill my duty.

· He told me that he was much obliged to you.

· Teachers have obligations towards their students.

· Students often feel obligations to their teachers.

I believe that global citizenship is the key to shaping our future because it helps us create a sense of <u>belonging</u> to a common humanity, creating a fairer world and hence helping learners to feel <u>obligated</u> and responsible to be active global citizens.

civic, involve

・He involved himself in civic action.

・The work involves being away from home a lot.

・Her moods are often involved with her physical condition.

・I was so involved in extracurricular activities that I ended up failing the exam.

This is a form of <u>civic</u> learning that <u>involves</u> students' active participation in projects that are just global issues of an environmental, political, social, or economic nature.

発展的課題

A．クェイ・ヤイさんがここで提起している「グローバル市民教育」を日本の学校教育の中に取り入れるとしたら，どのようなかたちが考えられますか？　具体的な授業プランを提案してください。

B．クェイ・ヤイさんがここで提起している「グローバル市民」という概念は，「世界市民」や「国際理解」といった概念とどのように異なりますか？

【コラム】 ■ ■「地球市民」アイデンティティーの持ち方？ ■ ■

　突然ですが、「私は＿＿＿＿＿です。」という文を 20 個作ってみてください。どのような文が並ぶでしょうか。

　「アイデンティティー」というのは、自分はどのような者であるかということについて自分が持っている概念ですが、周りと自分とを区別できるような特徴を含めて考えられます。加えて、自分と同じ特徴を持っている人は「仲間」であると捉え、同じアイデンティティーを共有するということにもなります。

　アイデンティティーには「個人的アイデンティティー」「社会的アイデンティティー」「超越的アイデンティティー」の３種類があります。「自分は個人としてどのような者であるか」という自己認識が「個人的アイデンティティー」、「自分は社会の中でどのような者であるか」という自己認識が「社会的アイデンティティー」であるといえ、それより巨視的な見地から見た自己認識が「超越アイデンティティー」となります。先程作っていただいた 20 文の中のいくつかは、多分「私は大橋理枝です」や「私は大学教員です」というような、自分個人がどのような人間であるか、ということに関わるタイプの文だったのではないかと思いますが、これらは「個人的アイデンティティー」を表した文だといえます。一方、「私は日本人です」や「私は放送大学に所属しています」というような、自分が社会の中でどのような立場にいるかということに関わるタイプの文、すなわち「社会的アイデンティティー」を表した文も、いくつかあったのではないかと思います。それでは、「私は人間です」や「私は地球人です」のような、巨視的な見地から見た内容の文は、いくつあったでしょうか？　多分この３つのタイプの中では最も少なかったのではないかと思います。

　アイデンティティーは対比されるものがあるとより強く意識されます。「個人的アイデンティティー」は、誰か他の個人と対比することで——つまり「私

は（小橋絵里などではなく）大橋理枝という人物である」という自己認識を
持つことで——意識化されますし、「社会的アイデンティティー」はどこか他
の集団に所属している人と対比することで——例えば「私は（東京大学では
なく）放送大学に所属している人間である」という自己認識を持つことで——
より強く意識されます。（だからこそ、日本にいると「自分は日本人である」
ということを意識することはあまりないのに対して、外国に行くと「自分は
日本人だ」ということが強く意識されることがあるといえます。）「超越アイ
デンティティー」についても同様で、「自分は人間である」という「超越アイ
デンティティー」は、人間以外の存在と対比した時に最も意識されると考え
られます。そうだとすれば、例えば動物に囲まれた時や、ＡＩ搭載のロボッ
トに囲まれた時などに「自分は人間である」ということがいちばん意識され
そうです。逆に言うと、「自分は人間である」という超越アイデンティティー
は、そういう場面でないとなかなか意識されないかもしれません。

　それならば「自分は地球市民である」というアイデンティティーは、どの
ような場面で最も意識されるのでしょうか？　理屈としては、「地球市民」
ではない他者と対峙した時に、最も強くそのアイデンティティーが意識され
るはずだと考えられます。そうだとしたら、それはどのような場面でしょう
か？？　宇宙人と対峙した時？！

　「地球市民」というアイデンティティーを持つことが難しいのは、この地球
上で生きている私たち自身を外から眺めることができないからというのもそ
の理由のひとつになりそうです。

（大橋理枝）

Chapter 15

Conversation with Shaney Crawford

Shaney Crawford has degrees in Linguistics, Education, and Library and Information Science. She is from Canada and, despite the fact that she only planned to stay in Japan for one year, has now lived there for over twenty years. While she has yet to find a satisfactory answer to the question of what she wants to be when she grows up, she has found direction and inspiration as the principal of Tsukuba International School, a job that combines the delight of working with children with just enough complexity to keep her attention for the past ten years.

K: Thank you so much for coming and joining us today, Shaney. Could you first give our listeners a just a bit of information about your background; who you are and what you do?

S: Sure. My name is Shaney Crawford. I am the principal of Tsukuba International School[1]. I'm originally from Canada. I've been in Japan . . . well, I originally came in 1995 and I lived in Fukushima for five years, then I went back to Canada for a little bit and I came back to Japan in 2002 and I've been living in Tsukuba since then.

K: Wow. So in total how many years have you been living in Japan?

S: I think that if we add it all up it comes to around 23 years at this point.

K: That's fantastic. Wow. What originally brought you to Japan?

S: So I originally came because I was in university and I had done a gap year[2] between high school and university. What that means is, I took a year off. In Canada, you can defer your application. So it means that I was already accepted to my university which was Queen's University[3] in Canada. And I

1）茨城県つくば市にある幼小中高一貫の国際バカロレア認定校。3歳から18歳まで、約272名（2020年9月現在）、約25の国につながる児童生徒が在籍している。〈https://tis.ac.jp/jp/〉

2）中等教育修了後大学進学までの間に、ボランティア活動などをして世間を知るために取る休業期間。

3）オンタリオ州キングストンにある大学。1841年設立。2019年秋学期で学生数25,260（学部生・大学院生を含む）、教職員数9,571（総計）。〈https://www.queensu.ca/〉

was able to therefore be ready to be enrolled the next year and take a year off. And what I did was I went to England and I worked in a boarding school [4] for a year, and that experience was so much fun. It was so eye-opening for me as a person, as a young person. I was 19 at the time, so pre-Internet. So, you know no research that I could do ahead of time to go to this tiny, tiny, tiny little village in England and, what happened was, I got the travel bug [5] so badly from that experience that when I was at university, every single year, I was like, "I need to travel, I need to go somewhere, I need to, . . ." but I was able to convince myself not to travel until I finished my degree. At the end of the first year, I'm like, "Can I go somewhere?" Second year, "Can I go somewhere?" But I was able to kind of rein it in. But during my fourth year, especially when I was working on my final exams. I was like, "I've got to get out of here." And I started to look for different places that I can go and could go and I applied to go to France and to Russia, and to Japan. And I was also about to apply to go to India. And I had a really great interview going to France but I made the mistake of saying that I wanted to get better at my French so that I could teach English in France. And they didn't like that answer. They wanted me to get better at French so I could teach French in Canada. And so I think I had an amazing interview and then I saw them,

---

4) 寄宿制の学校、学校の寮
5) 旅行に夢中になること。bug は何かに夢中な人や熱狂している人を指す。

they're like, "Oh yes, yes, great answers, great answers," I could see it on their faces. And then I said that and they were like, "Incorrect!" They didn't say that, but that's how it felt. And so I feel like I failed that interview based on that one wrong-headed statement. Anyway . . .

K: It was destiny, though,

S: It was destiny.

K: because you were supposed to come to Japan.

S: Apparently. I was supposed to come to Japan. And in fact, I applied to the JET program [6] to get here and I was put on a waiting list [7] . I was not chosen right from the get-go [8] . I don't know what they saw in me or didn't see in me to think that I wouldn't be a good person to come to Japan, but they were not right. I suspect I gave a poor interview again. But I was able to come to Japan as an English teacher and I was at the time 24 years old.

K: And this was on the JET program.

S: And this was on the JET program, and I was **assigned** to a really, really, tiny village in . . . not a village, sorry, a town in Fukushima prefecture at the time. Again, because there was no Internet, I could only try to find it on an atlas. And this town was called Tajima-machi, Minami Aizu-gun,

---

6）語学指導等を行う外国青年招致事業（The Japan Exchange and Teaching Programme）の略。外国青年を招致して地方自治体等で任用し、外国語教育の充実と地域の国際交流の推進を図る事業。〈http://jetprogramme.org/ja/〉

7）補欠になったということ。

8）「最初」という意味の極めて口語的な言い方。

Fukushima-ken [9], and I could find Fukushima. So I knew I was somewhere, I'm going to somewhere in Fukushima, but I really couldn't **figure** out where I was going even in the prefecture of Fukushima. So I just had to arrive in Japan and start looking at maps that were made in Japan to **figure** out where I was going to be in that prefecture.

K: Amazing how much things have changed since we first came here.

S: Um-hmm. Yeah, yeah.

I. Understanding the Contents

インタビューを速読して，問1～5に入る内容を，それぞれ a～d の中から選びましょう。

問1　シェイニーさんの現在の仕事は……

　　　a. 福島県のある町の英語教員

　　　b. つくば市にあるインターナショナル・スクールの校長

　　　c. JET プログラムの管理・運営

　　　d. フランス語教員

問2　大学生の頃のシェイニーさんは……

　　　a. 海外で生活することなど夢にも考えていなかった。

　　　b. ともかく海外に出たいと思いつつ4年間を過ごした。

9）福島県南会津郡にあった町だが 2006 年 3 月 20 日に舘岩村、伊南村、南郷村と合併して南会津町の一部となった。

c. ひたすら日本に行きたいと考えていた。

d. フランスにだけは行きたくないと考えていた。

問3　日本に来る際の採用面接でシェイニーさんは……

a. 1つ間違った答えをしたために不採用となった。

b. 絶好調でその場で採用された。

c. 補欠になった。

d. 福島県がどこにあるかを知らず顰蹙（ひんしゅく）を買った。

問4　日本に来たシェイニーさんの最初の仕事は……

a. 福島県の地図の作成

b. JET プログラムの教員

c. インターナショナル・スクールの教員

d. ボランティア活動

問5　赴任先の町のある場所をシェイニーさんは……

a. 実際に赴任してからも長いあいだわからずにいた。

b. 日本に来て日本製の地図を買って初めて知った。

c. 世界地図で調べて前々から知っていた。

d. インターネットのおかげですぐに確認できた。

II. The Opinions

インタビューの中の次の３つの部分を精読し，Shaney さんの主張をそれぞれ 100 字程度にまとめましょう。

Focus 1

S : So our personal definition of "international mindedness" which was created through a process of communal or community thinking involving the students, parents, teachers, board members[10], everyone. So we came together and tried to play out[11] the facets of "international mindedness," and we were able to bring it into these five points. So at Tsukuba International School, we believe that "international mindedness" is:

- Understanding, accepting, and **celebrating** human diversity.
- Having a sense of our own identity while respecting others regardless of their cultures, beliefs, or values.
- Engaging with the global community to gain a variety of perspectives and to foster a belief in our shared humanity and guardianship of the planet.
- Being able to communicate with empathy and compassion by speaking with our own voice, and listening with an open mind.

And finally,

- Being a responsible global citizen by making a contribution and taking action to make the world a better place for all.

---

10) 役員たち
11) ここでは最後まで考え抜くことを指す。

So in the past where . . . you know, in a classroom in an international school, for example, they might say "English only. You can only speak English. Don't ever let me hear you speak Japanese." That, you know, is like cutting off appendages for no reason. There's no reason to do that when that language can be used to aid in understanding, and to recognize that it's not that English is the best language, and the only language. It's that there are many languages, and English is just one of them. Your language that you speak at home is also extremely valuable. And you can use that to get at this other language, which is just another tool. English is another tool that you can use, and so not this . . . this idea of the superiority of one language over the other.

Focus 2

S : I think that English is the common language. I think there's no **arguing** that, that we, as Canadians, as English-speaking Canadians in particular, were just lucky. We just kind of won. We kind of won the lottery of the global language contest by speaking English. And I don't think that there's anything inherently good or great about English. It just historically happened that way, with the British Empire really expanding its hold—shall we say?—on the rest of the world at a particular time. That meant that English expanded the way that it did. So I'm quite agnostic in terms of whether it should be, or is, or whether . . . you know, whether it's a great language. I don't think that it is the best language because it's so complicated and has so many different exceptions. But the fact is that it *is* the global language. So what I would like to see happen is for other variations—shall we say?—on English to be accepted as equal. So, for example, you and I speak Canadian English. There's also American English and British English, but those are all examples of native speakers just having different accents, but I would like to see it where everyone agrees that those Englishes are at the same level as, for example, Singaporean English, Japanese English, Indian English—you know, any English from any country, and even—and this is a . . . this is a tricky one—for everyone, I think, languages . . . sorry, variations of the language spoken by native speakers differently. So, for example, African American English has often, in the past, been thought of as a lesser form of English. Or the Creoles [12)] that are spoken in certain parts of Central America, for example, or the Caribbean. Those are thought of as a lesser form of English. I would like it to be understood by more people that those are not lesser and that they are forms of English that are equally valid.

---

12) 本来は母語話者を持つ混成言語を指す語だが、ここではジャマイカ共和国をはじめとする幾つかの中南米の国で英語を基盤言語としたクレオール語が使われていることを念頭に置いている。〈https://www.mofa.go.jp/mofaj/kids/ichiran/i_latinamerica.html〉

III. Today's Vocabulary

以下の6つの単語について辞書を読み，さまざまな用例を理解した上で，
本文中での用例を日本語に訳してみましょう。

assign

・The task she assigned to me was very challenging.

・The date for the interview will be assigned shortly.

・They assigned the blame for the accident to the operator's lack of attention.

I was assigned to a really, really, tiny village in Fukushima prefecture.

figure

・He figured the cost to be over a million dollars.

・I figured myself living with him.

・I figured that you wouldn't come.

I really couldn't figure out where I was going. So I just had to arrive in Japan and start looking at maps that were made in Japan to figure out where I was going to be in that prefecture.

celebrate

Understanding, accepting, and celebrating human diversity.

Let us celebrate diversity. (Chapter 5)

engage

Engaging with the global community to gain a variety of perspectives.
I thought it would provide me with a good opportunity to engage in
extended discussions. (Chapter 10)

argue

· They kept arguing about the proper way to do the laundry.

· There's no arguing taste.

· She argued for his position in the council.

· He argued me out of carrying out the plan.

I think there's no arguing that we, as Canadians, as English-speaking
Canadians in particular, were just lucky.

inherently ← inherent

· Wild animals have an inherent fear of fire.

· Death is inherent in life.

· The responsibility comes inherently with the position.

I don't think that there's anything inherently good or great about
English.

発展的課題

A. 前章の発展的課題 A で, グローバル市民教育を日本の学校教育に
取り入れた場合の教育プランを考えました。つくばインターナショ
ナルスクールでのシェイニー・クロフォードさんの教育実践を踏
まえて, それを改訂してみてください。

B．日本の若者の「内向き志向」，つまり海外で学んだり働いたりする
　　ことを嫌がる傾向が問題とされることがあります。もしそのよう
　　な傾向を克服していく必要があるとすれば，どうすればよいでしょ
　　うか？　この授業でインタビューした5人の人々が日本に来た動
　　機を振り返りながら，考えてみましょう。

C．英語を準国際公用語として用いることの意義と問題点について，
　　この授業の中でさまざまな意見に接してきました。全体を振り返
　　り，今あなたは英語を学ぶことの意義をどのように捉えているか
　　述べてください。

【コラム】 ■ ■ **Global Citizenship** ■ ■

Creating and developing this course and textbook with my colleagues has been a wonderful experience, and it has given me a precious opportunity to reflect on the importance of global citizenship in my own life. Having lived in six countries, and having explored more than fifty countries, I have always considered myself to be a global citizen because of my travels, but the discussions in this course have opened my eyes to other factors that are just as important—if not more so—in making a person a true global citizen.

Firstly, the interviews we conducted for this textbook raised the issue, time and again, of making personal connections with people from different cultures and language backgrounds. Meeting people and making friends from other areas of the world breaks down the borders between us, and underscores the things we have in common. The more interconnected we become, the more effectively we can help and support each other.

Secondly, the TED Talks brought up issues related with respecting diversity and valuing other perspectives. Whether it is through the different naming practices in other countries or the varied ways of describing and relating information through our language systems, the TED speakers drove home the importance of recognizing that there are different ways of seeing the world—and some of them may even work better than our own.

Lastly, the readings showed the value in adopting English as a Lingua Franca, but also supported the evolution of World Englishes and the protection of existing languages. All our languages are important, and English should not be a system to replace other languages, but rather work as a tool to help us communicate. Each language and culture is special and valuable, and multilingualism is far preferable to monolingualism, so let's shed our insecurities and use the language skills that we are acquiring. Wherever we live, whatever our age, whenever we start studying languages, this gift of global citizenship is at our fingertips!

(Kristie Collins)

Appendixes

（インタビュー全文）

※斜体部分は放送教材では扱っていないところです。
（立体部分の中の斜体語は日本語の単語）

Appendix 1 : Navid Sepehri

K: Thank you so much for coming to talk with us today Navid. Would you be able to give us a little information about yourself and what you do?

N: Thank you very much for having me here. And I'm very happy that I can be part of your project. So my name is Navid, my family name is Sepehri-Amin. And . . . I'm from Iran and, well, I came to Japan in 2008 March . . . end of March . . . and since then I've been here. I never lived in any English-speaking country, 【**K:** Uh-huh.】 and, like, coming to Japan was my . . . maybe first country that I started living out of Iran. 【**K:** Wow.】 And I've been . . . like, actually practically living with my family all the time before coming to Japan. So it was kind of the first experience 【**K:** Wow.】 that I live by myself and in a foreign country.

K: Wow, that's really cool. Now when you first came to Japan were you expecting to stay here for a long time?

N: No. Like, there is a movie of me saying goodbye to my parents and . . . I just told them "Okay. See you soon." and "I will be back home in three years." So . . . it never happened.

K: So, yeah. So that would have brought us to 2011. OK. So what made you stay?

N: Well, actually, first was job. 【**K:** Um-hmm.】 So my . . . my research and my goal for future research and career. So I started my PhD here and I never expected that I will just stay in Japan . . . even during my PhD I was looking about different choices, different opportunities. And . . . well . . . life continued, and, like, I got my PhD degree, I saw that I am still successful in the place that I was doing my research, and all facilities enabled me to do whatever I wanted to do. And . . . like, more important than that, I met my current wife, **[K:** Um-hmm.**]** my wife, in 2008 I met her, and we were always together. **[K:** Yeah.**]** Although she was always fine to move anywhere with me, **[K:** Um-hmm.**]** but we ended up continuing living here together.

K: That's wonderful.

N: Thank you.

K: And so what do you study, or what were you studying? And what do you do now?

N: So, my res . . . my . . . my major is material science. **[K:** OK.**]** So I'm material scientist and my PhD is on magnetic materials. **[K:** OK.**]** It is more like material science and applied science and combination of that with physics and very old metallurgy sometimes is included.

K: Yeah, and so you're employed here in Tsukuba.

N: Yeah, yeah, yeah. So I . . . after my PhD I was post-doc for a couple of years **[K:** Um-hmm.**]** and I joined a research program called International Centre for Young Scientists and it's kind of tenure track position, and after that I got permanent position in NIMS and now I'm principal researcher in NIMS, National Institute for Materials Science in Tsukuba.

K: Fantastic. And so that's a governmental agency?

N: That's right.

K: Yeah. Very cool. Okay. What languages can you speak and where and when do you use them?

N: So, my mother's tongue . . . is Farsi, so I kind of speak Farsi and I can speak a little bit of English and also very little of Japanese. And very little of Arabic.

K: You are very modest. And here in Japan, where do you have a chance to use those different languages?

N: Well, English is my language at work. And also I still communicate with my wife in English. We started communicating with each other in English and it continues forever. [**K:** Right.] Although sometimes I change it to . . . like, my wife also can speak Farsi and she is Japanese, Japanese is her mother's tongue. And sometimes we speak to each other in Japanese, but that is not so often. [**K:** Okay.] So . . . but since my daughter was born . . . in, like, 4 years and a half ago, she . . . well, I was very concerned about language for her and I studied a bit about it and I like to speak to her in Farsi, but when my wife is around she doesn't change between Farsi and Japanese. She listen to me in Farsi, most of the time she answer me in Japanese. [**K:** OK.] So . . . that's why I'm learning a lot of Japanese from her as well. New words and new words.

K: That's great. Yes, I do need to borrow her more. And so at work, is everything in English? Or do you have to use any Japanese?

N: That's right. Everything is not in English, but some of my . . . like, I have foreigner students and postdocs. So with them I always use English and recently that . . . like . . . I'm more involved in some project, national projects or some collaboration with Japanese industries, I need to also use my Japanese capability. [K: Right, right.] So, sometimes I communicate with people in Japanese, it's becoming faster [K: Yeah.] than communicating with them in English. [K: Yeah.] And also I attend lots of . . . like, domestic conferences and workshops that [K: Right.] the main language is Japanese. [K: Right.] So I need to use Japanese as well.

K: Yeah, I think it's interesting that your first language is Farsi, [N: Yeah.] and your wife Keiko's first language is Japanese and that you speak to each other in English. [N: That's right, that's right.] I think that's really cool. And so at home Niki is . . . your daughter is actually getting access to three languages.

N: That's right. Sometimes that we are like . . . talking with Keiko like . . . very simple example, like where can we go for dinner? And we just say that in English. [K: Yeah] And Niki answer where she wants to go for dinner and like, "Okay, how do you know what we said?" [K: Yeah.] And, "I know what you're talking about." and she's catching. [K: So fortunate. Yeah.] She's actually smart.

K: That's great. I think it's also interesting that Keiko decided that she wanted to learn Farsi.

N: That's right.

K: So what motivated that for her?

N: Well, I think . . . well, my father kind of speak English, my mother to some extent, [K: OK.] not much, and she wanted to communicate more with them, [K: Right.] particularly my mother. And apart from that, . . . eh, . . . well, . . . her major is more related to, . . . like, her major is social science, [K: Um-hmm.] but her bachelor's degree was more related to language. **[K:** OK.**]** And she has interest, so she studied, and I was very happy **[K:** Yeah.**]** even though I was not with her at that time. **[K:** Yeah.**]** She was in Iran by herself with my family, **[K:** Which is awesome.**]** and . . . like, I really enjoyed that. When I saw her "Oh, she speaks lots of Farsi," **[K:** Yeah.**]** and I'm very happy.

K: And, and, and I'm sure that . . . that effort on her part really, really must have meant a lot to your family.

N: That's right.

K: Yeah, that's so cool. And now how about for you speaking with her family? What language do you use?

N: Yeah, I speak Japanese with them, and in the beginning it was like . . . it's too complex, my case.

K: I think it's fantastic!

What languages did you study in school in Iran?

N: *So main language was Farsi.* **[K:** *OK.***]** *So I never . . . taken any course in English in Iran.* **[K:** *Wow.***]** *So everything was in Farsi. And the time that I dec . . . well . . . the time that I first . . . like, I really need English was when I was writing my first scientific paper in English,* **[K:** *Wow.***]** *and I found that I'm very bad in English. So I started studying, but not for that particular paper. So studying English became more serious for me when I decided to go abroad* **[K:** *Hmm.***]** *for continuing my education, and I wanted to take TOEFL exam,* **[K:** *Right.***]** *and that was the serious time* **[K:** *Yeah.***]** *that "Okay. I need to study English."* **[K:** *Yeah.***]** *I studied.*

K: *And that was for graduate school?*

N: *That was during my graduate school.*

K: *During graduate school. Okay, so you did your master's in Iran?*

N: *I did my undergrad and master in Iran,*

K: *Okay, and then came for your Ph.D.*

N: *And came for Ph.D. abroad, yeah.*

K: *So how about . . . like today's kids who are going to school in Iran, are they only studying in Farsi, or are there a second language requirement?*

N: *We have English, but they . . . [K: OK.] they also do Farsi, in Farsi, [K: Um-hmm.] but we have English courses. [K: OK.] So from junior high school education of English starts, and I was going to after school programs to learn English as well, but it was never serious. [K: OK.] Although my parents were preparing environment for me to learn, [K: Um-hmm.] like going to class or so, but I never felt I need it, like . . . unless I decided to go abroad. Okay now I want to [K: Wow.] study abroad and I need English. [K: Right.] That's why, a second language.*

K: *So it was sort of seen as just a subject, not as a tool.*

N: *That's right, [K: OK.] that's right.*

K: *Is that still the case, do you think, in Iran?*

N: *I think it changed a lot. [K: OK.] So . . . well, I haven't been in Iran since 12 years and half ago, so I . . . well, I, I visit my family [K: Yeah.] once a while, of course, once a year, once per 2 years or so, [K: Yeah.] but I haven't lived there since long ago, so I don't know exactly what's happening. When I . . . but when I see, for example, my nephew or nieces, [K: Um-hmm.] I can see that they are*

studying and they are communicating with Keiko in English, like
fluently. [K: Cool!] So I feel like they . . . maybe it's my family that
they see that there is a foreigner that they're communicating with
them, [K: Yeah.] or I don't know what the reason is, but I can see
that the new generation, they are using it more often, [K: Yeah.]
so there is a change.

K: *That's really interesting. And I think it is . . . I think it's really*
interesting that having the opportunity to meet somebody outside
their culture can provide that motivation, [N: That's right, that's
right.] that's like, "Hey, we want to be able to talk to Keiko".

N: *Yeah. That's right.*

K: *Very cool.*

K: What do you see as the future of language communication in the
world of science?

N: I don't think there will be a big change. **[K:** OK.**]** So I think
English will remain **[K:** Um-hmm.**]** as the common language
for communication in science field **[K:** Yeah.**]** and worldwide.
Well, however, there is a possibility with the current growth of
economy **[K:** Um-hmm.**]** in some countries and considering the
population of, for example, China or so, **[K:** Um-hmm.**]** those, like,
some particular languages like Chinese **[K:** Right.**]** can play some
major role **[K:** OK.**]** in the future as well. But in terms of common
language in science community, **[K:** Yeah.**]** I think English will . . . ,
like, will be **[K:** Yeah.**]** the one.

K: I suppose especially with the internet and just this . . . um . . . having . . .

having this . . . in the cloud, research library of all of the writing in English, it's probably hard to reverse that now.

N: I think so. [**K:** Yeah.] I think so.

K: I would agree. So what advice would you give to young people who want to become scientists in this increasingly global society?

N: Hmm Well, I want to talk a bit more about this question, [**K:** OK.] because I came through this pass. [**K:** Right.] So as you realize from this interview, if you listen my conversation, not reading the text, you see that I am not that fluent in English. So I was never shy to speak English. [**K:** Um-hmm.] I know that I have lots of mistakes. I have lots of grammatical mistakes, I have lots of mispronunciation of the words that I'm saying. But Kristie, as native speaker [**K:** Yep.] can completely understand me, what I'm saying.

K: A hundred percent.

N: So I'm not embarrassed of mispronouncing any word and remember that if you are speaking English as your second or third language, you need to remember that you are more powerful than a person who speaks one language even though if that is English as mother's tongue. So you should not be embarrassed of, or shy, to speak the second language. If you are speaking second language with lots of mistakes, [**K:** Yeah.] it means that you know more than one, [**K:** Yes.] but it's good, it's positive.

K: Such an important message.

N: So, please, . . . please just have the communication [**K:** Yeah.] and that make you a stronger, to . . . to be able to . . . speak better and better, so nothing with practice gets better. **[K:** Yeah.**]** So it's something like a sport. You start with very bad . . . for example, I started tennis recently. I started with very bad . . . hitting the balls, and I'm getting better and better. So, why not? So please, please use it. And another thing that I would like to mention here. So assuming that after getting your undergrad degree, you want to enter even domestic company **[K:** Um-hmm.**]** in Japan. So even in that case. you are a stronger if you know English **[K:** Um-hmm.**]** or any second language, or third languages as . . . your . . . addition in your . . . in your CV. Because most of companies are not . . . it . . . it's hard to have a company as a domestic company anymore, because there is international collaboration, international business, international trade. **[K:** Right.**]** and you need to show your capability, to not only you have some knowledge, **[K:** Um-hmm.**]** major, in particular field, you are able to communicate and collaborate with other peoples all over the world. **[K:** Right.**]** So this is another plus for you. So, again, this is another motivation that **[K:** Yeah.**]** I would certainly encourage you to learn and use it in your daily life. Just for fun. Even with your friends you can use it. **[K:** Yeah.**]** Why not. And . . . er . . . the third option is assuming that after your undergrad degree you want to go for . . . for example graduate school. **[K:** Um-hmm.**]** And that time again, you definitely need English because you need to collaborate with different universities in the world, **[K:** Right.**]** you may go to different countries for continuing education or exchange programs **[K:** Yep.**]** or so and so forth, that can even happen during your undergraduate study. And that is another plus for you that you know different language. So I think . . . and . . . and the other thing is, when I see . . . well I know among young people that they are so eager to enter particular companies that they have great salary, nicer, like, kind of salary they can earn also, so people who can speak in different language and also they have some expertise in particular major or field, **[K:** Right.**]** I think many companies are very positive about them. **[K:** Yeah.**]** So all of these examples are I think . . . I hope it's motivating enough for you.

N: I have a project that I'm collaborating with the company **[K:** Uh-hmm.**]** in the United States **[K:** Um-hmm.**]** and just . . . I want to tell you that their company is located at the United States. **[K:** Yeah.**]** But among the colleagues that we are collaborating, only one person is native speaker.

K: That's so cool!

N: So this is . . . I think the simplest example **[K:** Yeah.**]** that many people in the world, **[K:** Um-hmm.**]** they are speaking English as second or third language.

K: Definitely. **[N:** So, . . . I think this is . . . **]** It's even the majority. Like, the . . . the . . . who . . . somebody like . . . myself, as a native English speaker, I'm a minority of the English-speaking community now. **You** are in the majority group. And I think it's really important to be hearing it from . . . from people like yourself, to . . . to have that advice that, you know, this is going to give you the opportunity to participate on a world stage. And, you know, as somebody from Iran—growing up with Farsi as a first language—coming to Japan to do the PhD and now using English globally with 【N: That's right.】 people on . . . on different scientific projects. 【N: That's right.】 It shows the power of communicative competency. It's exciting.

N: Language fluency helps you to have a easy communication. 【K: Right.】 But I would call it language communication capability. 【K: Yeah.】 So, language communication capability open me to new cultures 【K: Um-hmm.】 and that was really . . . kind of exciting. And also I started enjoy my life more. So let me . . . I said some example in terms of communication my in-laws . . . like my . . . my parents-in-law. And I feel much closer with them and I can understand them much more 【K: Right.】 because we can directly communicate with each other. Although I'm not fluent in Japanese, but I can communicate with them. 【K: Um-hmm.】 And . . . well . . . English, of course, it brought me to a very broad kind of community of the world and I'm . . . it's really nice that . . . the first international conference that I attended, I could feel "Oh, very nice that I can speak this language." And people don't mind . . . like if you have lots of mistakes 【K: Yeah.】 as long as you're clear what you are expressing and 【K: Right.】 what we are saying, that's enough. 【K: Um-hmm.】 And even if you are not clear, people try to understand what you are saying.【K: OK.】 That is also enough. 【K: Yeah.】

Appendix 2 : Louis Irving

K: Thank you so much for coming and speaking with us today, Louis. Can you tell us a little bit about who you are and what you do?

L: Okay, my name is Louis. I am assistant professor in the College of Biology at the University of Tsukuba. I am from Scotland, but I've lived in Japan for the last 13 years and I've worked at Tsukuba since 2010. I came to Tsukuba to start our G30 program, which is an internationalization program aimed at increasing the number of international students studying in the University. Our goal with that program was to open degree programs which are taught in English and to attract students from all over the world.

K: Tell me, what . . . what . . . what actually led you to Japan in the first place?

L: Um . . . so . . . when I was doing my PhD, I became interested in a particular protein in plant leaves called rubisco. And it's the . . . it's the enzyme which fixes carbon dioxide in photosynthesis. **[K:** Wow.**]** And it's the most abundant protein in the world. **[K:** OK.**]** And I was very interested in this, this protein, and how it influenced plant efficiency or plant productivity. And the best place in the world to study it is in Tohoku University in Sendai. **[K:** OK.**]** So I wrote to the professor at Tohoku University and said, you know, "Hey, can I come and visit you for . . . for a little while?" And he said, "Sure, if you can find funding." **[K:** Uh-huh.**]** And I wrote to my research council in the UK and said, you know, "Hey, I'd like to go and do this." And they said, you know, "Sure, here's a couple thousand pounds". **[K:** Wow.**]** And so I came across, and it was . . . I think my second time of ever being overseas. **[K:** That's amazing!**]** Yeah, the first time I went to Russia for a month. **[K:** Wow!**]** Yeah, I don't do things by half . . . by half. So . . . so I came to . . . and I was in Sendai for 10 weeks and I was really nervous because I knew nothing about Japan. **[K:** Uh-huh.**]** This is despite the fact that I'd actually studied karate for . . . since I was 15 years old.

K: It was destiny.

L: And you know, I'd done Japanese martial arts for years, **[K:** Wow.**]** but I actually didn't really know anything about Japan. **[K:** OK.**]** It was really, really far away, mysterious place. **[K:** Uh-huh.**]** And I came here and I found it such an interesting place. **[K:** Um-hum.**]** Everything was not quite understandable, **[K:** Um-hum.**]** and I really like that, you know, I liked having, I suppose kind of that little daily challenge, **[K:** Right.**]** learning new things about this very different culture to my own, and . . . so I did that during my PhD. After my PhD we applied for funding so that I could come back and do a postdoc **[K:** OK.**]** in Japan and we didn't get it. So I actually got a job in New Zealand. **[K:** Oh!**]** So it was my third country. **[K:** Wow.**]** So I'm going further and further away every time. And so I went to New Zealand and I worked there for two and a half years. When I was in New Zealand, the lab in Sendai sent me an email and said, you know, "Look, apply for funding." **[K:** Cool.**]** And I came back . . . I came to New Z . . . sorry, I came back to Japan initially as a . . . an English teacher **[K:** Um-hmm.**]** working for Nova, R.I.P. **[K:** Really?**]** Right. It was actually in 2007.

[K: OK.] So it was just at the time when Nova went bankrupt, [K: Oh my God.] so I worked there for six months, I got paid three times.

K: Okay, very twisty road.

L: Yeah, it's really bizarre, because . . . so I did that because there was going to be a gap between finishing my job in New Zealand and starting my position in Japan. [K: OK.] So I had to apply for funding and there was going to be a six month or a one year gap, [K: OK.] whatever I did. So I said, "Okay. Well, do I go back to the UK for six months or do I just go to Japan [K: Right.] and teach English for six months [K: Yeah.] and then do this?" [K: Wow.] And that was the decision I made. And so . . . yeah. So I was in . . . in Sendai for two years, and then none of my experiments worked, everything just blew up, everything died. And when I was there one of my colleagues came to me one day and said, you know, "Here's this job advertisement, you should apply for this," and I looked at it, and I said, "University of Tsukuba? Where's that?!" Never, never heard of this place before and I nearly didn't apply. [K: Wow.] Because I looked up Tsukuba online and I found out, you know, it's the Science City and there's lots of foreigners working there. And I thought, "Well, they probably already have an internal candidate." So I nearly didn't apply, because I thought, you know, I'm . . . I'm not going to get the job. And I put my application in the last day, and I forgot my recommendation letters. So, "Okay, it's over." [K: Wow.] A few . . . a couple of months later, they called me for an interview, [K: Uh-huh.] and I was devastated because I was . . . I was certain I wasn't going to get the job. So I thought,

"Now I need to go and buy a suit. I need to go and get, you know, *Shinkansen* tickets, [K: Right.] and I'm gonna have to get a hotel, and it's going to be three days, and it's just going to be a waste of time and money." And I came and I had the interview and they offered me the job right on the spot.

K: Oh, wow! That's fabulous!

L: So I was . . . yeah, it was kind of amazing . . . you know, turn of events. [K: Yeah.] Like . . . I couldn't believe it when they were like, yeah, "We like you, we're not interviewing anybody else." [K: Wow.] And I stood there for, like, about three minutes, like, turning this over in my head, like, "What does that mean, exactly?" [K: They accepted you at face value.] And eventually I thought, "Okay . . . ."

K: That's amazing. So clearly it was in the stars. You were meant to come to Tsukuba.

L: I guess so, you know.

K: So what made you stay?

L: I think it was the program and the students. I really found that this idea of internationalization is . . . I think it's an important idea [K: Um-hmm.] for Japan. Japan is going through a lot of changes at the moment. [K: Right.] The world is going through a lot of changes because of coronavirus and many other things. But Japan is an aging society, it's the oldest society on earth, [K: Right.] and this means when you've got a shrinking population of young people then that has implications for . . . for universities first of all, but then also for society as a larger thing, you know. You have more old people who need hospitals and doctors and social security, and you've got a shrinking workforce, and an aging workforce. So Japan is coming under increasing pressure in these ways. And I think that it's important for Japanese people to be able to become part of a bigger world for young people to be able to go and study overseas or for Japan to be able to welcome foreign people to work here, **[K:** Definitely.**]** and so those are societal changes which have to occur. For me, I think probably it's maybe a smaller and more compact reason than this is, we had these students come in from all these different countries and they were dreamers in a way. These were people who had a big dream for their lives and they loved Japan since they were young and they came here and they wanted to have this adventure and . . . and seeing how they changed over the period that they were here and seeing the lives they're leading since many of them have graduated, is . . . it's really fulfilling. **[K:** It is.**]** It kind of makes you realize that you . . . that what you're doing matters. **[K:** Yes.**]** *It's quite nice for me when I travel—not so much anymore, but here, before this year, when I would then travel overseas to go and visit high schools and . . . in the US or other places, you know, my graduates who are living in those places would send me an email and say hey, let's go and have dinner,* **[K:** *Yeah.***]** *and you'd catch up and find out* **[K:** *Yeah.***]** *what they've been doing and how their lives have been changing.*

K: *Yeah, it's . . . it's wonderful, isn't it? Like I* **[L:** *Yeah.***]** *I take such pride in the accomplishments of our graduates and I . . . I've been* *delighted to have them share, you know new jobs and to get in* *touch and say like "Hey, I'm coming to Japan!" and . . . and just* *seeing what an impact it's made, having that experience studying* *overseas, and yeah, and I think they bring that with them and you* *know this . . .* it doesn't end after the degree. You know, that that's a lifelong . . . lifelong learning experience.

L: I grew up in a small town in Scotland. My dad was a farmer. When I was in high school, we had to study a language, and the language I was allocated was French. **[K:** OK.**]** I was not an enthusiastic French learner. To this day, the only things I can say is "Je m'appelle Louis," my name is Louis, and "J'ai onze ans," I am 11 years old. Those are the only things that have stuck, everything else is gone. But my reason that it never stuck was because my goal in life was to be a farmer. I was never going to go to France. I was never going to go overseas. What's the point in learning foreign languages if you're going to live your whole life in one place? Since coming to . . . you know, and then since then, you know, I've traveled all over the world, and I've lived in New Zealand, I've lived here, and it changes you so much, and if you told me when I was 15 years old, "Louis, one day you will live in Japan and you know you will you work at a Japanese university, you will own a house in Japan, you will have a wife and a child." If you'd told me the things that actually happen to me, I would have laughed at you. I would have thought you are insane. And I look back at me when I was young and, you know, I wasn't a bad guy at all, but I was so narrow-minded. My world was so tiny. And traveling and meeting people from around the world has just widened my world. It's made it so much bigger and so much better and my life is something I could not have imagined when I was fifteen or sixteen years old. So, you know, learning different languages, traveling, living different places, is . . . there's . . . it's invaluable. It's amazing. Everyone should do it.

L: I think when we're talking about shyness, I mean that's definitely a big factor, and public speaking doesn't need to be speaking to, you know, a hundred people in a room. It can be speaking one-on-one with somebody. I know that when I speak in Japanese whether I speak in Japanese really depends on who I'm speaking to. If it's somebody I don't know, I'm far more likely to speak in Japanese. **[K:** Me too.**]** If it's somebody which I do know, somebody whose opinion matters to me, I'm probably more likely to be a little bit shy. **[K:** Yeah.**]** *I've seen the situation where I'm teaching in a lab class, and I have . . . one of my master students is a dual national Japanese-American and she was acting as TA in my class and there was a Japanese student and they didn't understand something I was trying to explain to them. So I switched from English to Japanese but right at that moment my graduate student came over, and my Japanese fell to pieces. It . . . it just . . . just went away.*

K: *Whereas you would have been fluent had she not come in.*

L: *I would have been totally fine, obviously. It's . . .* **[K:** *Yeah.***]** so the nerves are a really big thing, the . . . the fear of being judged. **[K:** Yeah.**]** So I try and tell the Japanese students especially that I don't care if they make grammatical mistakes at all. I don't care. Grammar mistakes, spelling mistakes, it doesn't matter to me. I care that they try. **[K:** Yes.**]** Because you have to try. **[K:** Yep.**]** Otherwise, you can either try or you can give up. Those are your two options and if you give up then you . . . you never get better at anything. **[K:** That's right.**]** So, fear, yeah, I think that's part of it for some of them. I think they went through high school and they've been studying English for a long time. **[K:** Um-hmm.**]** But they've never seen the point of it. **[K:** Yeah.**]** So they never they never really internalized it, they never really . . . it was . . . it was something to pass an exam **[K:** Um-hmm.**]** to get into university, **[K:** Right.**]** to get into something else. And I think that we only use the things that we actually feel are valuable. **[K:** Um-hmm.**]** And so I study Japanese because I live in Japan **[K:** Um-hmm.**]** and it's useful for me and my day-to-day. But if I wasn't living here I probably wouldn't see value in **[K:** Yeah.**]** studying it.

K: So we need to make it, like, real to them, **[L:** Right.**]** and have application outside of textbook.

L: Absolutely. You know English . . . I think if you're a Japanese person living in Japan you can probably live a very comfortable life without ever speaking English. You can go and watch subtitled movies, your news is delivered to you by NHK or whatever. You know, if you don't travel abroad then you're not going to need English, and even if you do travel abroad, well, you can go to Hawaii, **[K:** Yeah.**]** where, you know, there's . . . there's so much Japanese **[K:** Yeah.**]** support anyway, or Guam. These places which are very structured towards the Japanese tourist **[K:** Yeah.**]** industry. But again, you know, if you want to see outside, if you want to live in that bigger world, then being able to speak English is hugely valuable. **[K:** Um-hmm.**]** It opens so many doors to you. And I think this is perhaps where young Japanese people suffer as they don't see . . . they're kind of in the position I was when I was you know, 12 years old, **[K:** Yeah.**]** where . . . where the world is one way **[K:** Yeah.**]** and they don't realize it's much bigger. **[K:** Um-hmm.**]** But we can't . . . we can't describe colors that we don't have a word for. We can't imagine colors we don't have a word for. **[K:** Right.**]** We're limited by the language that we have, always, and there are words which exist in Japanese which don't exist in English because there are concepts which exist in Japan which we don't have in . . . in Western countries. And the same is true the other way around. **[K:** Right.**]** So language and culture are incredibly tied together. You can't understand Japan without understanding Japanese and I'm not sure that you can understand the UK or America or Australia if you don't speak English, at least to some level. **[K:** Yeah.**]**

Appendix 3 : Xiaoyin Wang

K: Alright, thank you so much, Xiaoyin, for coming and . . . and letting us interview you today.

X: Thank you for having me. Nice to see you.

K: Thank you. Likewise. 〖**X:** Yeah, yeah.〗 Can you tell us a little bit about yourself, who you are, and what you do?

X: Okay, my name is Xiaoyin Wang. I came to Japan about 20 . . . I guess 26 or 27 years ago, in 1994, yeah, so I've been living here for that many years. And first of all, I went to Hiroshima University with my husband and I had my Master's course there. And after graduation my husband had a chance to go to Canada to had his Ph.D. studies . . . a postdoc, to study. So I went there with him and stayed for . . . for maybe half a year, but he stayed for one year. 〖**K:** OK.〗 And I came back to Japan because he had a job here at Tsukuba University. 〖**K:** Uh-huh.〗 So that's why I came back to Japan with my family and since then . . . I think it was 1998. And since then I have been staying in Tsukuba, 〖**K:** Wow.〗 and I love here. 〖**K:** Me, too.〗 Yeah. I don't want to go anywhere else, yeah.

K: That's so interesting. But when you first came to Japan were you expecting to stay here and to, you know, have . . . have a life in Japan?

X: Well, honestly speaking, no. It wasn't my plan to come to Japan, actually. 〖**K:** Yeah.〗 I had always wanted to go to a . . . a native English-speaking country 〖**K:** OK.〗 because I majored in English at university, 〖**K:** OK. Wow.〗 and it was like everybody's dream to . . . to want to go abroad to study [**K:** Right.] at the time, you know. China had just opened to the outside world [**K:** Yeah.] at that period of time, and I had wanted to go to either . . . you know, US or Canada [**K:** Wow.] or, you know, Britain, [**K:** Right, right.] these places. But what . . . it so happened that my husband had a chance to study in Japan, [**K:** Right.] at Hiroshima University with a math professor [**K:** OK.] that he admired a lot, so [**K:** And so doing . . . doing math studies.] yeah, PhD study, yeah. So he came here and . . . so, not long after he came here, he brought me and the kids here. [**K:** OK] So I came here. When I came here, I didn't know any Japanese. [**K:** Wow.] So I was like . . . oh, of course, it's not true. I knew, you know, "arigato gozaimasu" and [**K:** Basic *aisatsu*.] I probably knew, yeah, "konnichiwa", things like that, [**K:** OK. Wow.] basic *aisatsu*, but I didn't know any Japanese.

K: Oh my goodness. And so you already had your girls in China? How old . . . how old were the girls when you took them here?

X: They were four, maybe? Yeah, three or four years old.

K: Wow. That is a brave move, taking twin four-year-old daughters [**X:** Yes.] to a country where you don't speak the language. [**X:** Right, right, yeah.] Wow. [**X:** Yeah, they were . . .] Did you enjoy it? Was it a good fit when you when you went to Hiroshima?

X: Well, of course it was, because, you know, I never thought about coming to Japan, but after I came to Japan—well, not long—I found that this is the place for me. [**K:** Oh, that's . . .] And I wanted to stay here longer. I wanted, you know, to . . . to know more about the people and the culture and this country. And then I just totally fell in love with this country. I didn't want to go anywhere else.

K: Oh, that's really great! So I know that you actually have become a Japanese citizen. **[X:** Yes.**]** When did you make that decision? And how did you make that decision?

X: Okay, that was about ten years ago, maybe a little more than 10 years ago, before I bought our house . . . we bought our house. Because, you know, in order to take the loan, **[K:** Right.**]** you know, mortgage, you would have to either have a Japanese citizenship or permanent resident, **[K:** Right.**]** yeah, right, yeah. Because we were . . . we were, yeah, torn in between whether to get a permanent residency or Japanese citizenship. **[K:** Right.**]** But you know, my husband is a . . . is a university professor and he has to go abroad to have, you know, joint research **[K:** Right.**]** and meetings a lot. **[K:** Right.**]** So if we get a permanent residency, he's still going to have a Chinese visa . . . a Chinese passport. **[K:** Passport. Right.**]** And then whenever, wherever he goes, he has to take visa, and it's such a . . . **[K:** It's expensive.**]** yeah, it's such a headache, **[K:** Yeah.**]** you know. You have to . . . it's not only expensive, he has to go to Tokyo, he has to **[K:** Ah . . . yeah.**]** get interviews and stuff like that and sometimes it takes time **[K:** Yeah.**]** and the meeting will be over by the time he gets the **[K:** Right.**]** visa. So we decided to get **[K:** Wow.**]** the citizenship, right. **[K:** Congratulations!**]** Thank you.

K: Now, does that mean . . . are your daughters full Japanese citizens, or dual, or Chinese?

X: No, actually my daughters . . . they can, you know apply for

Japanese citizenship. They could, at the time, apply Japanese citizenship with us. **[K:** Right.**]** And actually we had prepared to that and the documents were all ready. But in the beginning my daughters decided . . . at the time they were at the university. They were, like, thinking about this decision, and they decided to cancel that. **[K:** Wow. Interesting.**]** Right, yeah, they did. **[K:** That's cool.**]** Because . . . what . . . but now I can tell you, one of my daughters, the after she got a job **[K:** Right.**]** in Japan, she decided to apply too. So she is now Japanese citizen. **[K:** Wow.**]** Now, the other one hasn't applied.

K: Isn't that interesting!

X: It is. Because they decided . . . they told us, "Mom, we have thought about this for a while, and we . . . it's not that we don't want to, it's just that we are too young to decide, you know, we need to have more experience and we need to know more about **[K:** Of course.**]** Japan and, you know, the pros and cons **[K:** Right.**]** about this, and we are going to decide by ourselves later." **[K:** Wow.**]** Right. So they didn't.

K: I think that's really impressive. And, interestingly, my family, we were raised with two citizenships because my parents were American and we were living in Canada. **[X:** Um-hmm.**]** So we all had American and Canadian. And . . .

X: Dual citizenship **[K:** Dual citizenship.**]** were allowed?

K: Yep, between the US and Canada. **[X:** OK.**]** and it's just in the last three years, four years, that my parents and I have actually officially given up our American citizenship.

236 English for Global Communication

X: Yeah, I heard about that.

K: But my brother remains . . . he's living **[X:** OK.**]** in Chicago, **[X:** Oh.**]** and he has his American, so he has dual, but he . . . for . . . like your husband, there's reasons why it just makes more sense for traveling for business and such to have the American. So I think it's . . . it's a very different world we live in now, **[X:** OK.**]** where **[X:** Right.**]** languages and passports and visas . . . it's, yeah, it . . . it's a complicated, complicated situation that all of us have to think through carefully, **[X:** I know. Right.**]** yeah. **[X:** Yeah.**]** Very cool.

Please tell me a little bit about what you do for . . . for your work here in Tsukuba.

X: Oh, okay. Well initially, I worked at Tsukuba City Hall as a translator. Actually, what they call was, when they . . . they hired me they . . . the title for this . . . this job was called Coordinator for International Relations. **[K:** Ha!**]** Yeah, that's right. I worked at Tsukuba City Hall for about five years, **[K:** OK.**]** and . . . first of all, they . . . they just wanted to hire somebody who could speak Japanese as well as English and Chinese, **[K:** Yeah.**]** yeah. So because there are foreigners visiting there and they wanted to take the procedures so they need a translator. **[K:** Right.**]** So initially, I was just doing the translator, **[K:** OK.**]** translating thing. And then after that, I got more and more involved with the city, like sister city **[K:** Um-hmm.**]** business, you know, I went to . . . well, I had a chance to visit the US and Canada and Shenzhen, China, All sister cities of Tsukuba.

K: Okay, and can you . . . can you tell us again? What would JISTEC . . . what does that stand for?

X: Okay. JISTEC stands for Japan International Science and Technology Exchange Center.

K: What are the main responsibilities for JISTEC?

X: We kind of . . . can only serve research institutes that have contract with us. **[K:** Um-hmm.**]** And . . . so mostly researchers from foreign countries. They come here to Tsukuba to do research. They usually don't stay that long, like two or three years at most. Some people, of course, get hired by the Japanese research institutes and they would stay, like Navid, **[K:** Right.**]** yeah. But other people mostly . . . they just stay for a couple of years, and they have language problems. **[K:** Right.**]** And, you know, in Japan it's quite difficult to . . . to do all these, you know, the initial procedures, without some help, so.

K: Such as?

X: Going to city office to register your address, **[K:** Yeah.**]** join the health insurance, renting an apartment, **[K:** Right.**]** yeah, and going to hospitals, **[K:** Yeah.**]** for example.

K: Yeah, it's genuinely a different experience if you have that support, **[X:** Right.**]** and, yeah, this is where having a communicative language community here, **[X:** Right. Quite different.**]** is really important, yeah.

X: Especially in the beginning.

K: Gosh, yeah, **[X:** Right.**]** and pointing out where they might want to find support and social connections, **[X:** Right.**]** yeah. I know . . .

I know that you and Anna have probably been there for the birth of hundreds of babies.

X: Oh, I don't know how many people, one year was like eight.

K: Do you feel like a person's personality 【**X:** Um-hmm.】 and/or self-expression 【**X:** Yes.】 changes when they shift between languages?

X: Well, . . . actually, I don't think a person's personality can change according to what language he or she is speaking, just taking me for example. 【**K:** Um-hmm.】 I think I'm . . . whatever language I speak I'm always me. 【**K:** OK.】 And I'm always the kind of . . . I mean, I'm not so loud, I'm a little bit shy, 【**K:** Uh-huh.】 and if I'm with a group of people, I'm not the one who speaks a lot. 【**K:** OK.】 maybe. So I don't think I . . . personality would change. But probably depend on what language I'm speaking I would probably behave a little differently.

K: Can you give an example?

X: For example, if . . . if we were having a meeting, if I'm having a meeting with a lot of Japanese people, and people can discuss about a topic, 【**K:** Yeah.】 and I would not be very active. I would not just speak up before being asked to, you know, 【**K:** Yeah.】 I would just keep quiet, 【**K:** OK.】 mostly, because it's, like, it's expected, right? 【**K:** Right.】 from Japanese culture. You are not to . . . to be, like, to showing up or things like that. 【**K:** Yeah.】 But if I'm with a Chinese group, I will probably do whatever I want to, 【**K:** Um-hmm.】 and speak up. 【**K:** Yep.】 Yeah, right? And if I'm with an English-speaking group, probably that too.

K: What language education advice would you give to newcomers to Japan? So if you're . . . you have people coming here for . . . let's say, for three or more years. **[X:** Um-huh.**]** What . . . what sort of advice would you give them, and . . . I wrote this thinking about their kids but maybe to them as well. **[X:** Um-hmm.**]** So for . . . for adult people coming here and for parent people coming here, what language education advice would you give, and also how about for Japanese parents considering language education for their children?

X: Wow . . . well . . . I'm not sure I'm in a position to give advice because I haven't actually done much to my kids' education in terms of languages. We're just . . . we just went naturally, you know, yeah, let it . . . .

K: But . . . but you made some good choices that seems to have worked out well.

X: Thank you. To Japanese, in terms of learning languages . . . I . . . I think if you want to . . . to, to learn a language you have to practice, right? **[K:** Um-hmm.**]** You have to get over your shyness, **[K:** Yeah.**]** at least, and don't think about perfectness. Just try to speak whatever you have learned. **[K:** Yes.**]** Try to use it, even if you are not using it in the right way, **[K:** Yeah.**]** gradually I think you will . . . you will get . . . get it, right? **[K:** Yeah.**]** Yeah, that's . . . that's one thing. And . . . and . . . and if . . . if I'm a Japanese parent and I want my kid to, for example, to learn a foreign language, I think . . . I would, if I had a chance, or if I have the resources **[K:** Right.**]** about money and, you know, financial resources, I will . . . I will . . . I will send that kid to a native-speaking environment. Back then, we didn't have an English speaker around us, and we were listening to the tape recorders, 【K: Yeah.】 you know.

K: Oh, I remember those days.

X: No videos, 【K: Yeah.】 no movies, 【K: Yeah.】 you know. 【K: Yeah.】 Nowadays you can . . . whatever you want, 【K: Yeah.】 you can find it, right?

K: Yeah, online, or . . . or through just people in your community. 【X: That's right.】 Yeah. So, does it come down to, maybe, the same advice, people who are coming here to Japan, 【X: Right.】 or Japanese parents wanting to have multilingual kids. 【X: Right, right.】 It's using it, right?

X: Yeah, it is using, and I . . . I want to say to people coming to Japan. Some people they would focus their attention on research. 【K: Yes.】 And they just . . . some people . . . they would try to avoid speaking . . . to Japanese people. They . . . some research labs, they are full of Chinese, for example, 【K: Yeah, yeah.】 they're full of . . . you know, people . . . even Japanese people can speak English, so they just use English. Or use their own language 【K: Yeah.】 without using Japan . . . Japanese, without learning Japanese. I think it's such a pity. 【K: Yeah.】 And if you are in that environment, you don't have to spend time go abroad to learn language. 【K: Yeah.】 You are here. 【K: Yeah. Such a great chance.】 Why don't you just take this great opportunity 【K: Yeah, yeah.】 to learn the language, right?

K: And . . . and with it comes the culture and the people.

X: Right, **[K:** Yeah.**]** right, to make friends, **[K:** Yeah.**]** making friends with Japanese people. **[K:** Yeah.**]** Right. That's basically what . . . what I learned . . . how I learned Japanese.

K: Yeah. **[X:** Right.**]** And I think that's, like, the greatest gift is just that we can . . . we can make friends. **[X:** Right.**]** We can understand **[X:** Um-hmm.**]** people so much more **[X:** OK.**]** the more languages we know. Yeah.

X: Yeah. I just find it such an advantage **[K:** Yes.**]** to know language . . . different languages **[K:** That's great.**]** to know people from different culture, you know.

K: It just makes life more rich.

X: Yeah, much more interesting.

Appendix 4 : Herb Fondevilla ①

K: Thank you so much for coming and talking with us today, Herb.

H: Thank you for having me.

K: Would you be able to just introduce yourself to our listeners and tell us a bit about you and what you do? 【**H:** Um-hmm.】 Thank you.

H: Okay, so my name is Herb Fondevilla and I'm currently a visiting researcher at Meiji University. So my research concerns art, contemporary art, and . . . um . . . arts and health which is not very common, and I also do some research on arts and its benefits in persons living with dementia.

K: Wow, that's really cool. Now, where are you from originally?

H: I'm originally from the Philippines. 【**K:** Cool.】 I was born and raised in Quezon City.

K: Cool. Philippines is beautiful.

H: Thank you.

K: How long have you been living in Japan?

H: It's funny you ask that because, as I mentioned earlier, I came to Japan thinking I would stay for two years, and now it has been 15 whopping years.

K: It's amazing how time flies.

H: Indeed. I never thought I'd stay this long here in Japan, but you know here . . . here we are, and here I am. Still here.

K: It happens to all of us, it seems. 【**H:** It does.】 What brought you to Japan and what . . . what made you stay?

H: I came to Japan on a scholarship. I received a scholarship from All Nippon Airways.

K: Hah! I did not know that. 〔**H:** Yeah.〕 Okay.

H: So most people come to Japan in Japanese government scholarships. 〔**K:** Right.〕 I came on an All Nippon Airways scholarship 〔**K:** Oh.〕 and I came here because I was very interested . . . I still am, actually, very interested, in Japanese pop culture and how it's influencing our lives in a contemporary culture, 〔**K:** Um-hmm.〕 and I came here to study that. 〔**K:** Wow.〕 And I thought I was just going to do my master's for three years, and then go back to the Philippines and work in advertising. 〔**K:** Wow.〕 But things happened, 〔**K:** Yeah.〕 and 15 years on I'm still here.

K: Can you tell me what languages do you speak? And where and when do you use them?

H: Yeah, that's very interesting. So I was born in the Philippines and we speak two languages. So we have two national languages, Filipino and English. So we use them both in education, in law, in media, almost everywhere. When I was growing up, I remember we had this school rule where you have to pay one peso for every Filipino word that you speak. 〔**K:** Oh my Gosh.〕 Yes, they were pretty strict about it. And I don't think it's very common.

K: And so it was to discourage you from using 〔**H:** Filipino. Yes.〕 your national language.

H: Yeah, one of the national languages. 〔**K:** Wow.〕 So because when I was growing up, I've also lived with my grandmother, and she spoke a dialect which is called Romblomanon. And so growing up, I would . . . I had to master Filipino, English and had to learn how to understand Romblomanon. And my mom is . . . she's half Chinese, so she also spoke to me sometimes in Chinese, though I never picked up Chinese. So growing up I had, like, I was surrounded by four languages. **[K:** Wow.**]** But I think this is very usual for many Filipino families, because Filipino and English you just really need to study them, but many families also have roots in other places, other provinces, other islands, so they always . . . they also use another dialect. So many kids in the Philippines grew up with at least three.

K: That is amazing. **[H:** Um-hmm.**]** Wow. Do you think now that there . . . there is sort of a hierarchy or a prioritization of English over Filipino?

H: This's interesting. Um, when I was growing up . . . now I have to reveal my age.

K: Still younger than me.

H: I know. But during, like, the 80s, English was very much in use, and I think 1987 the country ratified the . . . the new Constitution, which said that now our official languages are Filipino and English. And . . . but in the 90s there . . . there was a movement to actually use more Filipino, and I think that came from the media when they started dubbing a lot of shows **[K:** Um-hmm.**]** in Filipino. **[K:** Uh-ha.**]** So we used to get a lot of movies, cartoons, from the United States, everything was dubbed in English. So growing up, I didn't know where these . . . where these shows came from. **[K:** Right.**]**

I knew they were American. I knew there were . . . even anime, I thought anime was from the US [K: Right.] because everything was in English. [K: That's wild.] TV commercials were in English, um . . . the books that I read, the newspapers were all in English. [K: Wow.] And . . . but in the 90s there was a new movement to encourage people to use more Filipino. [K: OK.] And so I think the current generation, those kids who were born in the late 90s to early 2000s, [K: Um-hmm.] I think they grew up hearing more Filipino in the media [K: OK.] than when I was a kid in the 80s. [K: OK.] So there has been, I think, a shift [K: Yeah.] in the way that we use language now.

K: Okay, we're going to shift over and talk to you a bit about different languages and dialects, um, because of your background. Um . . . so, you know, I'm sure that . . . that the Philippines is similar to some of neighboring countries in Southeast Asia. So some countries have their own version of English that is spoken and understood by a large segment of the population such as in Singapore with Singlish. Does the Philippines have a similar sort of dialect of English?

H: I think so. Yeah, I think . . . so, historically speaking, we have Tagalog but . . . but the Philippines has a lot of regional dialects. [K: OK.] And . . . and the Tagalog being the language of, I would say, the northern provinces, people from other provinces don't think it's fair that, you know, the Philippines chose Tagalog as the base language of the national language. So technically speaking, the national language is Filipino. But Filipino is based on Tagalog, which is a dialect.

K: Okay. I didn't know that. So Filipino and Tagalog are not the same thing.

H: No. So when you say Filipino, it's Tagalog 【**K:** Uh-huh.】 with Spanish words in it, some English words in it, it's a mixed language. 【**K:** Wow.】 You can say it's like Creole. 【**K:** OK.】 So . . . but not many Filipinos know this technicality. 【**K:** OK.】 So when people ask me, "What is the national language of the Philippines?" I always say "It's Filipino," 【**K:** Yeah.】 because that's what's written in our constitution. 【**K:** Excellent.】 So.

K: And I genuinely, like, I would have said, if somebody said, "What is the language of the Philippines?" I would have said, "Tagalog," and it's not.

H: No, it's not. It's Filipino.

K: New information!

H: With an F. 【**K:** Uh-huh. OK.】 It used to be spelled with a P and then they changed it to F.

K: Why?

H: To recognize our background, you know, 【**K:** OK.】 as having had Spanish, and American, and, of course, a local language thrown in, so . . . to emphasize that, you know, this is a mixed culture, a mixed language, 【**K:** Wow.】 so. But however, other people would say, it's not fair that the country based 【**K:** Yeah.】 the national languages . . . the national language, on Tagalog, 【**K:** OK.】 wherein there are languages such as Cebuano or Hiligaynon and they don't think it's fair. If you go to the Philippines you may notice that some Filipinos don't even want to speak Tagalog. They don't . . . they don't accept it.

K: That's fascinating. Are they . . . are they so different that people wouldn't understand [**H:** Yes.] each other?

H: That's true, yeah. If I go to the Northern parts of the Philippines, I . . . I don't understand Ilocano at all. [**K:** Wow.] It's . . . it's like going to different countries, it's like German to me or something.

K: Wow. So it's the same writing system.

H: Um . . . yes, we use the . . . the alphabet.

K: OK. So everybody can read each other's language, [**H:** Yes, but they cannot . . .] but they cannot necessarily understand it. [**H:** understand it.] Fascinating. Wow. So . . . so what was your . . . your dialect growing up?

H: So when I was growing up, of course, I had Filipino, my grandmother spoke Hiligaynon, or Romblomanon, which is another dialect, my mother spoke a little bit of Chinese to me. But this is . . . she . . . the province, is from Fukien, it's not Mandarin. [**K:** OK.] So it's a different Chinese dialect as well. [**K:** Wow.] And then of course it's English. When I think about it, the most . . . I would say, the most stable language in my life has been English.

K: Wow, that's . . . that's really fascinating. I find . . . whenever I'm on Facebook or social media [**H:** Um-hmm.] and I see Filipino . . . Filipino friends writing that I can understand some of the comments but not all of them, [**H:** Yes.] because there seems to be a lot of mix [**H:** Yes.] and English popping in everywhere. [**H:** Yes.] So is that . . . would you think of that as a . . . like, distinct separate dialect?

H: Um . . . people . . . this is a lot of like . . . I've heard a lot of discussions **[K:** Hmm.**]** about it. So I would say in the 80s, there was one of the daughters of the former president Corazon Aquino, her name was Kris Aquino, and she made it, I would say, trendy to speak English and Filipino mixed together. **[K:** Wow. OK.**]** And . . . but at the same time it became a language that the upper class would use. **[K:** Ha.**]** So if you want to sound like a member of the, I would say, member of the **[K:** Of elite-ish?**]** upper class, **[K:** Uh-huh.**]** the elite, you would use this language, and it's funny how . . . and of course the people from the lower classes dislike this, **[K:** OK.**]** because they are . . . or for some people who are not able to speak in just one language **[K:** Um-hmm.**]** they would mix it up. **[K:** Um-hmm.**]** I would say that, you know, I think it's just natural, **[K:** Yeah.**]** because we use so many languages in our everyday lives, it's just natural to mix them up. And I think you understand this because sometimes there are words that you just can't express **[K:** Right.**]** in English, but you know how to express it in Japanese. **[K:** Exactly. Yeah.**]** And that's how it happened in the Philippines. We speak . . . speak this Taglish, **[K:** Yeah.**]** Tagalog English, **[K:** Taglish . . .]** and that's . . . and most of the time it's people of the upper classes would speak this form of mixed Tagalog and English **[K:** So fascinating!**]** at the same time.

H: *[It] has been said that the Philippines is the Latin America of Asia. [K: Cool.] So our culture is a mix of Latin cultures. At the same time, we are still Asian, [K: Right.] you know, we do eat rice every day and we are horrified when rice is disrespected. And at*

the same time, as a former American colony, so we have English,
and we use it in our educational system, in . . . our laws are written
in English.

K: *That's just . . . that's just so fascinating. It's such a unique, unique*
culture really. Wow. Do you consider yourself a native English
speaker?

H: I consider myself as a bilingual native English speaker. **[K:** OK.**]**
So I can't say that . . . um . . . I am just . . . I would say . . . because
it's funny how people would . . . um . . . like, how they define what
is a native **[K:** Yes.**]** English speaker, because there are many
native English speakers, but they all speak in different accents. **[K:**
Right.**]** Right? So . . . um . . . a lot of Filipinos have been studying,
have been learning, have been hearing English, from the moment
they were born, **[K:** Right.**]** but they don't necessarily speak it
because it makes you sound like a snob if you just speak to people
in English, like, "Why are you speaking in plain **[K:** Yeah.**]** and
straight English to people **[K:** Yeah.**]** when it's not supposed to be
just your only language? **[K:** Yeah.**]** You're supposed to have at
least two."

K: Do you feel that outside of the Philippines that people perceive
Filipinos/Filipinas to be native speakers? Like, is this for you in
Japan? Do you feel that you are perceived as a native English
speaker?

H: No, I don't think so. And I think there's a hierarchy of how people
look at or define what native speakers are, and I think they define
them from where they are from, or their citizenship, mostly their

passports. **[K:** Yeah.**]** So, I would say that, um . . . but this is a very . . . it's really undefined, you know, because I would say that I have met so many people from India, from Pakistan, and they speak really good English because the . . . and I think they also consider themselves as native English speakers. We all just speak in different accents, **[K:** Right.**]** and you can't fault us because of globalization. I mean, if, um . . . if the . . . let's say, if the Americans, or if the British didn't want English to spread this far and wide, then they shouldn't have crossed the seas **[K:** Right.**]** and left us alone, right? But they did, and so this happened. But I think here in Japan, especially, when they think of what a native English speaker is, **[K:** Hum-hmm.**]** I think they would consider first what this person looks like. **[K:** Um-hmm.**]** Is this person the typical white person, **[K:** Hm-hmm.**]** you know, blue eyes, blond hair, and what country is . . . what country is that person from, are they from US, Canada, UK, Australia, and then it goes on and on. But the Philippines is kind of like at the bottom of the ladder, and I think that there are reasons for that, other than the Japanese idea of what . . . of what a native English speaker looks like. I think it's economics.

K: *Can you explore . . . explain that more?*

H: *Yeah. So in the '80s a lot of Filipinos came to Japan as entertainers. And so a lot of Japanese, especially those who are of a certain age,* **[K:** *Right.***]** *would . . . they have this idea that Filipinos are usually entertainers, they work in bars and clubs or . . . and also, um, many Filipinos work as nannies.* **[K:** *Um-hmm.***]** *Many Filipinos work in* *the United States and Canada, they work as nurses. So we have all of these default jobs **[K:** Yeah.**]** that Filipinos do, and so it kind of puts you in a position of privilege of being an English speaker, but not of the same level as a white, um, as a white native English speaker.*

K: *And it becomes a class, as you say.*

H: *So, it, but . . . It does.*

K: *Not white collar jobs. These are blue colored jobs.*

H: *Yes, so it's big . . . it's a class, **[K:** Yeah.**]** and, . . . and it's a racial issue as well. **[K:** Yeah.**]** So I think that things are changing now. Many Filipinos come to Japan to work as teachers. **[K:** Um-hmm.**]** And some of them work in the tech industry, but there's still the stigma and sometimes I do feel it.*

Appendix 5 : Herb Fondevilla ②

K: What advantages and disadvantages have you personally experienced with your unique linguistic background?

H: Advantages would be . . . in Japan, one of the better-paid jobs for foreigners is teaching English. **[K:** Right.**]** And ever since I came to Japan, you know, I started . . . I came here as a student, and I get 2,000 yen per hour for teaching English. If you compare that to working at a convenience store, that's 1,000 . . . what . . . 980 yen **[K:** Um-hmm.**]** per hour, and that's a lot of money. **[K:** Yeah.**]** It's a big difference. **[K:** Yeah.**]** The disadvantage would be . . . is that people still judge you from where you come from, and from what you look like **[K:** Yeah.**]** when it comes to jobs. **[K:** Um-hmm.**]** And it's interesting. I'm not sure if people have discussed this, but in Japan, and if you're a foreigner, and the better you are at speaking Japanese, **[K:** Um-hmm.**]** in a way you get more integrated into the culture, **[K:** Um-hmm.]** and there's . . . and the more pressure is put on you. And a lot of people, like, even for me I noticed that, that . . . the more you appear to not understand Japanese, in a way the better you are treated, and I think it's sometimes really strange.

K: What's behind that? Because I agree with you.

H: Even I am still like . . . I am, you know, because for me sometimes, like . . . they call it the *gaijin* card, **[K:** Right.**]** right? If you want to get out of trouble,

K: Play the *gaijin* card.

H: Play the *gaijin* card, **[K:** Yes.**]** because people treat you better if they think you are stupid **[K:** Um-hmm.**]** than if you try to assimilate. And you try very hard to speak Japanese, and then they treat you worse because you speak Japanese and because you understand Japanese culture. But at the same time, they have to understand, you are doing this to the best of your abilities, but you are still not Japanese, and **[K:** Right.**]** you still need help; "But I am trying my best, please help me." **[K:** Yea.**]** But if you're just, like, "I don't care about your culture.", **[K:** Yeah.**]** I'm just gonna speak whatever language I can use, **[K:** Yeah.**]** and you, you know, just do what you can . . . **[K:** Yeah.**]** I don't understand it either.

K: Yeah, it is. It's so interesting that there seems to be kind of these different levels of fluency that we reach when we've **[H:** Yes.**]** stayed here and tried to invest in learning and . . . and there's . . . in the beginning if you can you . . . if you can do a couple of *aisatsu* . . .

H: It makes me afraid, you know.

K: And if your *hashi* are *jozu* . . .

H: Yeah, I know, I was like, what . . . it's . . . chopsticks.

K: Yeah, and, and, and, at that point you get so much praise for just such basic kind of Japanese. But then, yeah, the . . . the more advanced you get, **[H:** Yes.**]** there's a turn.

H: Yes. This is like, you reach this level and then suddenly they don't like you anymore, and it's like, "What?!"

K: Or at least you're no longer . . . you're no longer going to get the assistance **[H:** Yes.**]** because now you're on your own.

H: I know, and it's 【**K:** Yeah.】 really strange to me, 【**K:** Totally.】 because I thought that, you know, people would treat you better, because they understand that . . . they know that you understand Japanese already.

K: And that you're investing in 【**H:** Investing in Japan, yeah.】 trying to learn. Yeah.

H: But at the same time, you know, there is some . . . I think there are so many things in Japan that still don't make sense to me even after 15 years. One of them is apartments. 【**K:** OK.】 So looking for an apartment, my experience was that if we . . . when I moved to Yokohama I had to go to a real estate agency and asked them if I could rent this apartment. 【**K:** Right.】 The first thing the real estate agent did was to call the owner and tell them that a foreigner wants to rent an apartment. 【**K:** Yeah.】 And most of them, I would say 90%, said no. 【**K:** Awful.】 And then I would tell them . . . "Tell, tell the owner that I speak Japanese", and then your odds, you know, like, go up, 【**K:** Yeah.】 maybe, maybe they will let you rent the apartment because you speak Japanese.

K: Yeah, show some responsibility. 【**H:** Yes.】 Yeah.

H: And I hear that it's because, you know, foreigners don't know how to take out the trash, they are noisy. they have parties, and stuff like that. But I think you know, these are just, again, presumptions 【**K:** Yes.】 that not all foreigners like to party and don't know how to . . . and don't care about taking out the trash. 【**K:** Right.】 Because, you know, if you, . . . you know, I have been here for 15 years. I am invested in this country, 【**K:** Yeah.】 and I do know how to take out the trash properly, and I don't have parties all the time in my house.

K: And locals may, you know, **[H:** Yeah.**]** it could be an issue that parties might be by local people.

H: And I think it's also because they have this . . . it's also because of the media. **[K:** Yeah.**]** Whenever foreigners do something bad, it's all over the news. **[K:** Yes.**]**

H: I have a very pan-Asian look. When I'm in the Philippines I look Filipino, when I'm in Japan I can pass as Japanese, but when I start speaking, **[K:** Uh-huh.**]** like "Oh, no." and then you can see them start to back away little by little from you, and . . . and . . . it has happened to me several times, you know, like I try to speak in Japanese, but of course my Japanese is not perfect and I have an accent when I speak Japanese. They know I'm not a native Japanese speaker, and you can see their faces turn and slowly back away from you.

K: Yeah. Yeah.

H: At least they talk to me. What are your experiences? They just . . .

K: It's interesting. Maybe it builds a case for . . . for having a global language. **[H:** Yes.**]** If we . . . if we all share one language, would that put everybody on the same playing field?

H: I think so. At the same time, you know, there are issues around it, **[K:** Yeah.**]** English as a global language, because it does speak of colonization.

K: That's really problematic, isn't it? Yeah.

H: The hegemony . . . the hegemony of Western cultures.

K: Yeah, because we are just already start the race close to the finish line. **[H:** Yes.**]** Yeah, so, cause, yeah, that's my last question. It's "Do you think it's a good idea to have English as a Common Language worldwide? Why or why not?" [sigh] **[H:** sigh**]**

H: I think it's a very loaded question. Um . . . personally, because I already speak English, it's good for me. **[K:** Um-hmm.**]** It's to my advantage to have English as a global language. I know how hard it is to learn, to master another language. Having studied Japanese and having lived in Japan all these years, Japanese is not an easy language to master. And even Japanese people themselves are still, you know, it takes an entire lifetime to master their own language. **[K:** Right.**]** I always tell my students, you know, the English alphabet only has twenty six letters, **[K:** Um-hmm. Very quick to learn them.**]** so much easier, **[K:** Yeah.**]** it's easier to look things up in the dictionary, **[K:** Yeah.**]** it's only 26 letters. But at the same time, if you go deeper into the issues, you know, this . . . like, what I mentioned, is the history of colonization. **[K:** Yeah.**]** The hegemony of Western cultures. At the same time . . . at this . . . at this stage in history, at this moment in history, how are we going to choose? What side are you on? Shall we speak English? Should we speak Chinese? Technically, there are more Chinese speakers in the world.

K: That's right.

H: At the same time, academic research; mostly in English. **[K:** Right.**]** Right? Um . . . .

K: And right now there are less . . . there are less first language native English speakers, then there are English as a second language **[H:** Yes.**]** or third language speakers. So when it comes to, like, dialects and . . . and Singlish, or, like, **[H:** Yes.**]** all these different things, there's more of them than native English speakers. **[H:** Um-hmm.**]** So in a sense, there's, like, well, maybe Chinese would make sense as there's more native speakers of that language.

H: At the same time, there's also an issue with Chinese, because there's traditional Chinese, **[K:** Right.**]** spoken in Taiwan or written in Taiwan. And of course, there's Chinese from China written in a . . . in a different system, you know. **[K:** Right.**]** And it's also . . . I would say even the Chinese themselves, they don't know which Chinese. **[K:** Yeah.**]** There are so many Chinese dialects as well.

K: Yeah, and also politically loaded **[H:** Yes, very politically loaded**]** with those different languages. So . . .

H: Shall we just go into Russian now? [laugh]

K: I've always thought we should go with Esperanto and have this artificial, created language that has no cultural backup.

H: But that would mean upending all the research that has been done in the past and all of the documents and all of the academic learning. **[K:** Yeah.**]** Do we translate them all to Esperanto?

K: Good question. Yeah, the internet seems to have fixed it. **[H:** Yes.**]** It's like, now that it is on the internet and everybody is connected that way, it's almost like English has become the de facto language.

H: In a way. And I think it's really because of you know entertainment, because of technology, and I would say a lot of influencers are English-speaking.

K: Yep. And maybe still a bit of . . . a kind of . . . elite image, for better or worse.

H: Yeah, I think so. It's a . . . it's a very interesting question. It's something that we all really need to think about, especially, you know, during these times, you know, it's a very politically loaded question [**K:** Yeah.] with a lot of historical and sociological, you know, background, you know, [**K:** It's true.] It's crazy, [**K:** Yeah.] but it's something . . . you know. Like, but, what I said, you know, if English is to become the de facto national . . . uh . . . like, language of the world, [**K:** Yes.] I wouldn't be against it, [**K:** Yeah.] because it is to my advantage. [**K:** Yeah.] and I would say that it . . . that it is to the advantage of every single person who has ever studied English as well. And, of course, for anyone who likes to watch movies, TV, you know, English is the most widely used language for entertainment. [**K:** That's right.] The internet, you know, music as well. [**K:** Yeah.] Popular music, I would say . . . that . . . soft power is really the thing that counts here; which country has the biggest soft power influence?

K: And what do you mean by soft power?

H: It means, you know, like influence by popular culture, entertainment, movies, music, things we didn't think were important [**K:** That's right.] until now! And now we look at everything. [**K:** It's currency.] It is the currency, like, it is more powerful than politics, I would say. Think of all . . . this is the reason why Trump didn't like all those TikTok users. Soft power, and all the youth culture.

K: So this is almost all in English?

H: Almost all in English. So I would . . . it's also the reason why, let's say, when it comes to soft power in south . . . southeast . . . sorry, soft power in Asia, the reason why South Korea is so popular right now; entertainment. Japan used to be number one, but they did not really support the anime industry. A lot of . . .

K: After the cool power, and then it just sort of went away.

H: After . . . aft . . . yeah, so they didn't really support the anime industry, a lot of people who work in the anime industry are poor, a lot of manga . . . [K: Um-hmm.] all of the content creators, they're struggling. But if you give them power the way, I would say, Hollywood actors and actresses . . . [K: Right.] people who work in the entertainment industry in other countries are given the freedom and the power and the money. [K: Yeah.] And you can see how much influence, you know, how they can turn the tides. And I would go look at Hollywood. I would go look at Cool Japan, how that turned out. I would look at K-pop right now. [K: Yeah.] and see, you know, like, how it has turned people, you know.

K: And . . . but with that . . . that sort of requirement, that it has to be made available to a global audience, which requires English . . . [H: Um-hmm.] at least in part.

H: It's . . . it's a very interesting case because when you think of K-pop [K: Um-hmm.] many of their K-Pop singers or idols also speak English.

K: I know, and . . . and, and . . . it amazed me just seeing some of them on . . . on late night interview shows. **[H:** Um-hmm.**]** Very fluent speakers, **[H:** Yes.**]** and a lot of their songs have a lot of English in it. **[H:** Yes.**]** And I, I think that they're attracting a much bigger overseas audience than ever before.

H: They're huge. They're huge in United States. Like my . . . my nephews and my nieces are . . . are all into K-pop, BTS. **[K:** Yeah. BTS is huge!**]** They don't even speak Korean. **[K:** Yeah.**]** But you know, they see them in interviews, they hear them speak English, and they . . . they can . . . and then they can relate to them.

K: Right. And Japan could totally be doing this.

H: Japan could be **[K:** Yep.**]** doing this, but I think . . . right now . . . the animation . . . the anime industry is changing in Japan. **[K:** Um-hmm.**]** The money is not coming from Japan anymore. A lot of Japanese anime are now being financed by overseas companies. **[K:** Hmm.**]** Companies . . . and a lot of anime in Japan are now being done offshore. **[K:** Wow.**]** Some of them are being done in Taiwan, and I think some of them were being done in South Korea. Anime is not just Japan anymore. **[K:** Yeah.**]** It's become, in a way, global. **[K:** Yeah.**]** The ideas are still very Japanese; the content, the main content creators are still Japanese, but a lot of labor that has been put into it . . . **[K:** Um-hmm.**]** Financing is coming from Hollywood, and companies from China are financing anime companies. **[K:** Wow.**]** So . . .

K: But that requires also communication skills, right? Yeah.

H: That will require communication skills, and most likely it will be

English. [**K:** Yeah.] Netflix is putting a lot of money into anime companies [**K:** Yeah.] and they will require, you know, subtitles, dubs. [**K:** Right.] And that is very interesting, I think . . . . . Let's wait 5 to 10 years. [**K:** Yeah.] Let's see how this will change. Pop culture as we know it, and we all . . . we both know pop culture [**K:** Yeah.] is one of the biggest influences of our time.

K: Definitely. Definitely. Perfect. Well, I think we're done. Thank you very much for your time.

H: Okay. Thank you.

Appendix 6 : Shaney Crawford

K: Thank you so much for coming and joining us today, Shaney. Could you first give our listeners a just a bit of information about your background; who you are and what you do?

S: Sure. My name is Shaney Crawford. I am the principal of Tsukuba International School. I'm originally from Canada. I've been in Japan . . . well, I originally came in 1995 and I lived in Fukushima for five years, then I went back to Canada for a little bit and I came back to Japan in 2002 and I've been living in Tsukuba since then.

K: Wow. So in total how many years have you been living in Japan?

S: I think that if we add it all up it comes to around 23 years at this point.

K: That's fantastic. Wow. What originally brought you to Japan?

S: So I originally came because I was in university and I had done a gap year between high school and university. What that means is, I took a year off. I had . . . in Canada, you can defer your application. So it means that I was already accepted to my university which was Queen's University in Canada. And I was able to therefore be ready to be enrolled the next year and take a year off. And what I did was I went to England and I worked in a boarding school for a year **[K: Cool.]** and . . . but that experience was . . . it was so much fun. It was so eye-opening for me as a person, as a young person who's . . . I was 19 at the time, so pre-Internet. So, you know no research that I could do ahead of time to go to this tiny, tiny, tiny little village **[K: Wow.]** in England and . . . but what happened was, I got the travel bug so badly from that experience that when I was at university, every single year, I was like, I need to travel, I need to go somewhere, I need to, and . . . so . . . but I was able to convince myself not to travel until I finished my degree. **[K:** OK.**]** At the end of the first year, I'm like, "Can I go somewhere?" Second year, "Can I go somewhere?" But I was able to kind of rein it in. But . . . at . . . during my fourth year, especially when I was working on my final exams. I was like, I got to get out of here. **[K:** Yeah.**]** And I started to look for different places that I can go and could go and I applied to . . . to go to France and to Russia. **[K:** Wow.**]** And to Japan and I was also about to apply to go to India. Um . . . and I had a really great interview going to France but I made the mistake of saying that I wanted to get better at my French so that I could teach English in France and they didn't like that answer. They wanted me to get better at French so I could teach French in Canada. And so I think I had an amazing interview and then I saw them, they're like, "Oh yes, yes, great answers, great answers", I could see it on their faces, and then I said that and they were like, "Incorrect!" They didn't say that, but that's how it felt. And so I feel like I failed that interview based on that one wrong-headed statement. Anyway,

K: It was destiny, though,

S: It was destiny.

K: because you were supposed to come to Japan.

S: Apparently. I was supposed to come to Japan. And in fact, so I applied to the JET program to get here and I was put on a waiting list. I didn't . . . yeah, I was not chosen **[K:** Wow.**]** right from the . . . from the get-go. I don't know what they . . . what they saw in me or didn't see in me to think that I would be a good person to come to Japan, but they were not right. And . . . I think . . . I suspect I gave a poor interview again. But . . . but yeah, I was able to come to Japan as an English teacher and I was at the time 24 years old.

K: And this was on the JET program.

S: And this was on the JET program, and I was assigned to a really, really, tiny village in . . . not a village, sorry, a town in Fukushima prefecture at the time. Again, because there was no Internet, I could only try to find it on an atlas **[K:** Wow.**]** And this town was called Tajima-machi, Minami Aizu-gun, Fukushima-ken, and I could find Fukushima. So I knew I was somewhere, I'm going to somewhere in Fukushima, but I really couldn't figure out where I was going even in the prefecture of Fukushima. So I just had to arrive in Japan and start looking at maps that were made in Japan to figure out where I was going to be in that prefecture.

K: Amazing how much things have changed **[S:** Um-hmm.**]** since we first came here.

S: Um-hmm. Yeah, yeah.

K: *So, what does global citizenship mean to you?*

S: *So, it's . . . you know, there's . . . there's sort of micro and macro level ways of thinking about global citizenship. The macro way, I think, is the one that people think about on a regular basis . . .*

the . . . you know, being a good . . . you know, being kind to the environment and, you know, making choices that . . . that . . . the small choices that you make having a big impact at the global level. But, I think, also the micro-level is something that we need to think about very carefully, and this is how I tend to think about it in terms of my school. So, at . . . at my school I tend to think about it in terms of the relationships that you have with each other and the friendships that you have and not necessarily because, for example, you know, I'm from Japan and you're from China or you're from Canada or not. Not that, but even the two of us, you and I, are both Canadians, and we think differently about some things. And if we, as two Canadians, can't have a different thought or a different way of thinking about something and work through it, [K: Yeah.] then there's no chance for international and global thinking to work at a bigger level. [K: Absolutely.] Right? So that's . . . that's how I think . . . I think of it, this, this tiny, micro-level where it's just "Can we get along?" [K: Yes.] up to the "Can we save the planet?" I think it has a massive spectrum.

K: *Yeah. Is it a term that you use with kids?*

S: *Yes. So in my school we call it "international mindedness". [K: Hm. OK.] I think it's the same . . . the same concept that we're trying to get at here today. And, in fact, because my school is an International Baccalaureate school, which means that it's a school that has gone through a process of gaining what we call authorization to offer the International Baccalaureate programs. Part of that is . . . part of that process is to define "international* *mindedness" and how we are all going to agree to think about it at our school. And so my school has this definition of "international mindedness". And what we try to do is to embed that into the learning. Not just say that, for example, there're students from this country and that country, you know, five different countries are represented in this class, therefore we are internationally minded. Not like that, but to say, in order for "international mindedness" to be taught and learned, it needs to be explicitly addressed in the classroom, in the events that we do, in the ways that we interact with each other.*

K: *Right. How ... so ... it sounds ... it sounds like a really ... not a simple concept but a clear concept but probably quite difficult to ... to actually put into action.* **[S:** Um-hmm.**]** *So, how do you teach global citizenship or "international mindedness" to your students and what values or actions do they connect with this concept?*

S: *So may I read out our definition?*

K: *Absolutely. That'll be great.*

S: *It's a little bit long, it's a five part ... five part definition,*

K: *That would be wonderful.*

S: So our personal definition of "international mindedness" which was created through a process of communal or community thinking involving the students, parents, teachers, board members, everyone. So we came up ... we came together and tried to play out the facets **[K:** OK.**]** of "international mindedness" and we were able to bring it into these five points. So my school's name is Tsukuba International School, so;

At Tsukuba International School, we believe that international-mindedness is:

- understanding, accepting, and celebrating human diversity
- having a sense of our own identity while respecting others, regardless of their cultures, beliefs, or values
- engaging with the global community to gain a variety of perspectives and to foster a belief in our shared humanity and guardianship of the planet
- being able to communicate with empathy and compassion, by speaking with our own voice, and listening with an open mind

and finally,

- being a responsible global citizen by making a contribution and taking action to make the world a better place for all

K: That's amazing.

K: *What role do languages play in being a global citizen?*

S: *So this is also a really, really important part of being an International Baccalaureate school and more recently, they have . . . in our . . . In our language policy, for example, we have to outline specifically how we are creating a more "internationally minded" student through the learning and the teaching and learning of languages. And they do . . . they used to say that the students, we should be trying to make students at least bilingual and now they are not limiting it and saying we want students to be multilingual. So it . . . which can . . . which encompasses bilingualness, [**K:** Right.] it can just be two languages, but this is trying to get at the point that many of our students, for example, will have home* languages plus the language of the country that they're in, which is Japanese, plus the language of instruction, which is English, *[K: Right.]* And . . . and a concept that is used quite a lot in international schools these days is translanguaging, *[K: What does that mean?]* which means . . . so traditionally in international schools or in schools where the children might be learning in a language other than their mother tongue, quite often the schools will say, "Yes, fine, you have that other language, but forget that for now, we are speaking English here. You cannot speak any other language. I'm not going to admit the existence of any other language as a teacher in this classroom." Whereas recently that thinking has changed to this concept of translanguaging which means using whatever languages you have in the room to try to get at whatever other language you're trying to teach. *[K: Wow.]* So, in the case of English, you know, if you've got some students in your class who speak Japanese, you know, in the past, and you know, I'm trying to think of a word that, you know, you're trying to get at . . . at the concept of "linguistics", *[K: Right.]* for example. Well, if you just say the word "linguistics" to some students, any age students, in English or Japanese, they don't really know what it is. *[K: Right.]* But if you can say "In Japanese, we say 'gengogaku'." Then . . . at least, "Oh, gengo. I know gengo means language. So this has something to do with language." and "Oh, oh I noticed as well, 'linguistics' kind of sounds like 'language'." *[K: Yeah.]* So it's using just any tool that you have to aid in understanding and processing and kind of the pairing of languages like that in your *mind.*

K: *And in that kind of context, are the students kind of encouraged to help each other?* [**S:** *Absolutely.*] *Yeah. So this is . . . this is helping each other to be able to raise awareness or comprehension.*

S: *Exactly.* So in the past where . . . you know, in a classroom in an international school, for example, they might say "English only. You can only speak English. [**K:** Right.] Don't ever let me hear you speak Japanese." [**K:** Right.] That, you know, we're . . . it's like cutting off, you know, appendages [**K:** Yeah, yeah.] for no reason. [**K:** Yeah.] There's no reason to do that when that language can be used to aid [**K:** Exactly.] in understanding, and to . . . to recognize that it's not that English is the best language [**K:** Yeah.] and the only language. It's that, you know, there are many languages [**K:** Right.] and English is just one of them. Your language that you speak at home is also extremely valuable [**K:** Yeah.] and you can use that to get at this other language, which is just another tool. [**K:** Right.] English is another tool that you can use, and so not this . . . this idea of the . . . what do you want to call it? The . . . the superiority of one language [**K:** Right.] over the other.

K: *Because this way, I mean, it would be ignoring the resources* [**S:** *Um-hmm.*] *of all those shared languages in the classroom,* [**S:** *Yes.*] *yeah.*

S: *Yes, exactly.* [**K:** *Wow.*] *So, you know, sometimes we have teachers who can speak Chinese or French or Spanish and they might say, for example, even if nobody in this classroom speaks French,* [**K:** *Yeah.*] *they might say, "Well, you know what? In*

*French we say it like this because . . . " and, you know, talk about it, so that students just get this idea that [**K:** Yeah.] language is this . . . this fluid thing, and this alive thing, and is used in so many different ways [**K:** Yeah.] and so many different cultures. Not that any one language is better than any other.*

K: *It's very empowering that way, I'm sure,*

S: *I think so. I think so.*

K: *that the students can see that this is like a skill set they already have.*

S: *I think so.*

K: *Cool. So, at . . . at Tsukuba International School, how many languages are taught there and from what age or year?*

S: *So we teach . . . so the classes are in English and as a second language, we teach Japanese from the age of three.*

K: *Wow, three.*

S: *So the students are . . . are . . . we're hoping the students can graduate from our school fully bilingual. It's . . . a lot of that depends on the child's motivation, the parent encouragement, etc., etc. But we have . . . you know, often or usually, if the child is of a Japanese heritage to start with, they can graduate as a bilingual student and gain the bilingual diploma from the International Baccalaureate. However, even in the case where a child comes to us at a younger age not speaking any Japanese, you know, we can often get them to the point where they can graduate with the bilingual diploma, [**K:** Wow.] and what that means is, they can write an essay in Japanese. [**K:** Wow.] To . . . and pass that essay,* you know, pass the . . . pass the . . . the exam so it means writing on the spot, writing an exam about Japanese literature in particular.

K: That's impressive. Do you think the students see connections between languages and "international mindedness"?

S: I hope they do, but I also know that students are . . . children are developmentally sometimes not ready to see big picture things. *[K: Yeah.]* So some very perspicacious students, very, you know, . . . students who are kind of really, really, in . . . really aware, might pick up on that but I wouldn't say that everyone gets that connection *[K: Yeah.]* as clearly as we might as adults. But they certainly will as they get older.

K: Do you think it is a good idea to have English as common language worldwide and why or why not?

S: So I think that English is the common language. I think there's a . . . there's no arguing that, that we, as Canadians, as English-speaking Canadians in particular, were just lucky. We just kind of won . . . we kind of won the lottery of the global language contest by speaking English and I don't think that there's anything inherently good or great about English. It just historically happened that way, with . . . with, you know, the British Empire really expanding its hold—shall we say?—on the rest of the world at a particular time. That meant that . . . that English expanded the way that it did. So I don't . . . I'm quite agnostic in terms of whether it should be, or is, or whether . . . you know, whether it's a great language for . . . or . . . I guess I would say I'm, I'm, I'm . . . I don't think that it is the best language because it's so complicated and has so many different exceptions. But the fact is that it **is** the global language. So what I think is . . . what I would like to see happen is for other variations—shall we say? —on English to be accepted as equal. So, for example, you know, you and I speak Canadian English. There's also American English and British English, but those are all examples of native speakers just having different accents, but I would like to see it where everyone agrees that those Englishes are at the same level as, for example, Singaporean English, Japanese English, Indian English—you know, any English from any country, and even—and this is a . . . this is a tricky one—for everyone, I think, languages . . . sorry, variations of the language spoken by native speakers differently. So, for example, African American English **[K:** Um-hmm.**]** is often . . . or has often, in the past, been thought of as a lesser form of English **[K:** Right.**]** or the Creoles that are spoken in certain parts of Central America, for example, or the Caribbean, those are thought of as a lesser form of English. **[K:** Right.**]** I would like it to be understood by more people that those are not lesser and that they are forms of English that are equally valid.

K: *Hear, hear. Thank you very much for your thoughts on all of these topics.*

S: *My pleasure.*

問 題 解 答

Chapter 1

I. Understanding the Contents
問1　d.　　問2　c.　　問3　d.　　問4　b.　　問5　d.

II. The Opinions
Focus 1

人の名前にラストネームが含まれるというのは万国共通のように思われがちだが、そうではない。ミャンマーにはラストネームという概念は存在せず、申請書などに記載することもない。

【全訳】

不思議だなって思いません？　ラストネームがなかったら祖先をどうやってたどるんでしょう？　私たちのほうでも、世界中のミャンマー以外の人々が、ラストネームがどうしても必要で、それを申請書類に必ず書き込まなければならないって主張するのが不思議だなって思うんです。ミャンマーの申請書類にはラストネームは必要ありません。そのかわりに、自分の名前を省略なしで記入し、それから父親の名前を省略なしで記入します。ミャンマー大使館が発行したこのビザ申請書類もそうなっています。

Focus 2

アジアの人間がグローバル社会で活躍するには、西欧風の名前を持っていた方が便利である。そのため生まれたときに西欧風の名前を子につける親が増えている。しかし伝統的な名前がそのために消えてしまってよいのだろうか？

【全訳】

Cynthia Win という名前はビジネスの世界ではたいへん重宝しますが、でもミャンマーにおいてきてしまった Shwe Sin という小さな頃の自分を思い出して寂しく思う気持ちも、私の中にはあります。シンガポールをはじめとし

てアジアの多くの国では、赤ん坊が生まれたときに、便宜のために西欧風の
名前をつける傾向が進んでいます。David とか Cynthia とか Linda といっ
た名前の子が将来増えるでしょう。そして Shwe Sin なんていう名前の子が
この世界にいなくなってしまうかもしれません。異なる文化の中での名前を
覚えて、そして誰でも文化に根ざした生まれたときに与えられた名前を使え
るように配慮しないと、「輝く純金のアカデミー賞」などという伝統的には
意味のある名前が、次の世代にはもう消えてしまうかもしれません。

III. Today's Vocabulary

recognize

Even I couldn't recognize my dad's name.

私は自分の父親の名前さえ（それが父の名前だと）わからなかったのです。

represent

Babies born on Monday will have names beginning with a set of letters
from the Burmese alphabet and a tiger represents them.

月曜日に生まれた赤ちゃんはビルマアルファベットの中の特定の文字から始
まる名前になり、虎がその象徴になります。

Wednesday is divided into morning and afternoon represented by elephants
with and without tusks.

水曜日は午前と午後に分けられていて、牙のある象とない象とによって象徴
されます。

share

Let me share with you how my name has evolved over the years.

さて、私の名前が年を追うごとにどのように変わっていったかについてお話
しさせてください。

adopt

In 2008 I went to Australia for graduate studies and decided to adopt a Western name.

2008年に私は大学院の勉強のためにオーストラリアに行って、西洋式の名前を名乗ることにしました。

register

I've grown so disassociated with my own name that it now takes me a while to register that is actually me.

私はあまりにも自分の本来の名前から切り離されてしまったので、今ではそれが実際に自分を指しているのだということに気付くまでしばらくかかるようになってしまいました。

Chapter 2

I. Understanding the Contents

問1　d.　　問2　d.　　問3　d.　　問4　a.　　問5　d.

II. The Opinions

Focus 1

英語のさまざまなバリエーションをどう扱うかという問題はネットの普及した1990年代から認識されるようになった。アメリカ英語の影響が絶大とはいえ、それぞれのバリエーションは固有性を保っている。

【全訳】

1990年代までには、英語を教える際に英語のさまざまなバリエーションをどう扱うかという問題が議論されるようになった。そして1993年に行われたパネル・ディスカッションの参加者たちは、今日でも論議されているような実

に多様な見解をすでに示している。1990 年代という時代は、問題の新たな複雑さについての認識が深まった時代だった。状況はもはやイギリス英語かアメリカ英語かという単純な問題ではなくなり、それ以外のバリエーションが強い影響力を持ち、そしてインターネットのおかげで、英語学習者たちはかつては考えられなかったようなかたちでそれに接するようになった。どの英語が最終的に主流となるかがしばしば問われるようになり、そしてたぶんそれはアメリカ英語だろうという考え方が広がった。いま言えることは次のようなことだろう。たしかに、アメリカ英語はさまざまな英語のバリエーションに絶大な影響を与えたが、しかしさまざまなバリエーションがその固有性を失ってしまったわけではない。イギリス英語は、一世代前よりアメリカ英語的な特徴を見せるようになったにせよ、それでもイギリス英語であることに変わりはないのである。

Focus 2

イギリス英語とかアメリカ英語といった伝統的な英語とは別の、国際英語が新たに生まれてくるのではないかという考え方も生まれ、そのための研究も進んでいる。しかし同時にネイティヴの英語を規範とすべきという考え方も残っている。

【全訳】

このような流れの中で、それまでとは異なる考え方が生まれてきた。つまり、伝統的な英語のバリエーションのうちにどれかひとつが支配的になるということはない、そうではなくある種の国際英語のようなものが新たに生まれてくるのだ——という考え方である。クロースはそれを「コモン・コア（共通の核）」と呼び、ネイティヴの話す英語とは区別した。グラドルは「どこかある特定の国で話されるタイプの英語を原型とはしない」英語が発達するとした。こうした問題を研究すべきだという認識が広まったのである。ある寄稿者は英語の国際的なデータを集めたコーパスの必要を訴え、これは現在では

英語国際コーパスやウィーンの VOICE コーパス（ウィーン・オックスフォード国際英語コーパス）というかたちで実現している。しかし何をもって範とするかという問題は依然として残っている。別の寄稿者は、国際英語について然るべき研究がなされるまでは、ネイティヴ・スピーカーの話し方を基準にすべきだと主張している。チェンはそのような基準をコミュニケーションに用いることができるようにしておくことの意義を強調する。

III. Today's Vocabulary
survive

It wasn't conceivable a generation before, according to Reg Close, thinking back to 1937: 'who could have imagined that English would survive as a *lingua franca* ?'

レジ・クロースによれば、1937 年にさかのぼって考えてみると、それは一世代前には考えられないことだった。「英語が共通語として存在し続けるなんて、誰が想像できただろうか？」

anticipate

Our present-day concerns are anticipated.

現在の我々の懸念は以前から言及されている。

Graddol makes the important point that diversity is nothing new: 'we have already learned to live with a pluricentered language', and anticipates greater tolerance of variety.

グラドルは、多様性は新しい概念ではないという重要な指摘をしている。「我々は既に複数の中心を持った言語と共に生きることを学んでいる」として、変種への寛容度がより高まることを予想している。

Graddol anticipated the development of an English 'not modelled on any one national variety'.

【Focus 2】全訳参照

remain

Many felt they would have a short life, or remain only as 'low' colloquial speech.

多くの人が、それらは短命であるか、単に「低位」口頭言語として残るだけだろうと感じていた。

The question of best practice remains.

【Focus 2】全訳参照

positive

The contributors are positive about increasing diversity.

寄稿者たちは、変種が増えていることに対しては肯定的だ。

evolve

Some sort of new international English would evolve.

【Focus 2】全訳参照

relevant

Chien emphasises the need to make these norms communicatively relevant.

【Focus 2】全訳参照

His comment on the role of the teacher is as relevant today as it was then.

教員の役割に関する彼の指摘は、今日でも当時と同様に当を得ている。

Chapter 3

I. Understanding the Contents

問1　b.　　問2　a.　　問3　c.　　問4　b.　　問5　c.

II. The Opinions

Focus 1

科学の分野では、今後も英語が世界共通言語であり続けるだろう。すでに膨大な量の英語による科学論文がインターネット上にある以上、英語が世界共通言語という現状を変えることはきわめて難しい。

【全訳】

K: 科学の世界で、言葉によるコミュニケーションの未来はどんなふうになると思いますか？

N: 大きな変化はないんじゃないでしょうか？

K: なるほど。

N: まあ、英語が科学の分野におけるコミュニケーションでは世界共通の言語であり続けるんじゃないでしょうか。とはいえ、現在いくつかの国で起こっている経済成長とか人口増加とかを考えれば、ほかの可能性もあります。例えば中国語がメジャーな役割を果たす可能性もあるんじゃないでしょうか。でも科学者のあいだでの共通言語について言えば、やはり英語が共通語になると思いますね。

K: そうですね。とくにインターネットのことを考えると……みんなクラウド上に入っちゃったわけですから。膨大な量の研究論文が。それがみんな英語で書かれてる。いまから［英語が共通言語という］現状を変えるのは難しいかもしれませんね。

Focus 2

英語を話す上で大切なことは、多少の間違いを気にしないこと。多少の間違いがあっても、第2言語を話すということは、誇りとすべきことである。

【全訳】

N: このインタビューを聞いていておわかりと思いますが、テキストを見ずに私の話だけを聞いていただけば、私がそんなに英語に流暢ではないことは

おわかりになるでしょう。でも私は英語を話すのが恥ずかしいとかまった
く感じません。たくさん間違いはあるでしょう。文法的な間違いとか、発
音の間違いとかあると思います。でもネイティヴであるクリスティーは、
完璧に私の言いたいことを理解してくれます。

K: 100 パーセント理解していますよ。

N: だから私は単語を間違って発音するのが恥ずかしいとか感じません。英語
を 2 番目あるいは 3 番目の言語として話している人間は、英語を母語とし
て話す人よりもその分だけ力があるということを理解するべきでしょう。
だから 2 つ目の言語を話すことを恥ずかしがったり照れたりするべきでは
ないんです。2 番目の言語を話してたくさんのミスをしたとしても、それ
は 2 つ以上の言語をあなたが知っているということを意味します。それは
いいこと、ポジティヴなことではありませんか。だからどうかどうか、コ
ミュニケートしてください。

Focus 3

ネイティヴ・スピーカーがたった 1 人しかいない国際的な研究グループの中
で、英語がコミュニケーション言語となっている事例からもわかる通り、ネ
イティヴ・スピーカーはもはや英語コミュニティーの中では少数派である。

【全訳】

N: 私はいまアメリカのある企業との共同プロジェクトに参加しているんです。
その企業はアメリカにあるんですが、プロジェクトのメンバーのうち英語
のネイティヴ・スピーカーはたった 1 人なんですよ。つまりこれなんかは
いちばんわかりやすい例だと思います。世界中の多くの人たちが……み
んな第 2・第 3 の言語として英語を話しているということですね。

K: その通りですよね。英語のネイティヴ・スピーカーである私は、英語を話
す人間のコミュニティーの中では、むしろ少数派ということになります。
あなたの方が多数派なんですよね。だからあなたのような方から、英語を

話すということが世界という舞台に参加する機会を与えてくれるんだというアドヴァイスを聞くのは、ほんとうに大切なことです。あなたは、イラン出身で、ファルシ語（ペルシャ語）を母語として育ち、日本で博士号をとり、いろいろなプロジェクトを通じて、グローバルに英語を使っていらっしゃるわけですから。コミュニケーション能力がどれほどの力になるかを示していますね。素晴らしいですよね。

III. Today's Vocabulary

motivate

What motivated that for her?

彼女がそうすることを動機づけたものは何だったのですか？

（なぜ彼女はそうしようと思ったのですか？）

remain

English will remain as the common language for communication in science field and worldwide.

【Focus 1】全訳参照

particular

Particular languages like Chinese can play some major role in the future as well.

【Focus 1】全訳参照

reverse

It's probably hard to reverse that now.

【Focus 1】全訳参照

embarrass

I'm not embarrassed of mispronouncing any word.

【Focus 2】全訳参照

You should not be embarrassed of, or shy, to speak the second language.

【Focus 2】全訳参照

Chapter 4

I. Understanding the Contents

問1　c.　　問2　d.　　問3　b.　　問4　d.　　問5　a.

II. The Opinions

Focus 1

今日、英語がグローバル言語になる一方、信じ難いスピードでさまざまな言語が消滅しつつある。この2つの現象は無縁ではない。それはともに開発途上国の近代化政策と先進国の経済拡張とによってもたらされたものである。

【全訳】

でも残念なことに、今日では、いまだかつてないスピードで、いろいろな言語が絶滅しつつあるんです。14日に1つの割合で、言語が消えています。その一方で、英語が議論の余地のないグローバル言語となりました。この2つの現象のあいだに繋がりがあるんでしょうか？　私にはわかりません。でもいろんな変化が起こったこと、それは私は見て知っています。初めてペルシャ湾岸にやってきたとき、私はクウェイトに来ましたが、その頃はまだクウェイトは生活に困難が伴う任地とみなされていました。そんなに昔の話でもないんですよ。その写真はちょっと古すぎますけどね。それでも私は、25人ほどの教員と一緒にブリティッシュ・カウンシルにリクルートされたんです。私たちは非イスラム教徒として初めてクウェイトの国立学校の教員になりま

した。私たちは英語を教えるために招かれました。それはクウェイト政府が教育を通じて国を近代化し、そして国民に力を与えたかったからです。そしてイギリスは、もちろんクウェイトの油田で大儲けさせていただいていたわけです。

Focus 2

英語がグローバル言語となったこと自体を批判しているのではない。それは現代大いに必要とされている。しかし言語の多様性もまた必要である。だから英語力で学力を測りそれを障壁としてしまうことには反対である。

【全訳】

誤解していただきたくないのですが、英語教員のみなさん、私は英語を教えること自体に反対しているわけではありません。英語がグローバル言語になったことを私は嬉しく思います。今の時代は、かつてないほどに、グローバル言語を必要としています。でもそれを障壁にしてしまうことには、私は反対します。最終的に言語の数が 600 に減ってしまい、そして英語があるいは中国語がメインであるという状態になって、それでいいんでしょうか？もっとたくさんの言語を私たちは必要とします。どこに一線を引くのでしょう？　英語の知識と知力とをイコールにしてしまうシステム――これはたいへんに横暴です。

III. Today's Vocabulary

unprecedented ← precede

Languages are dying at an unprecedented rate.

【Focus 1】全訳参照

undisputed ← dispute

English is the undisputed global language.

【Focus 1】全訳参照

empower ← power
The government wanted to modernize the country and to empower the citizens through education.
【Focus 1】全訳参照

benefit (v.), beneficial ← benefit (n.)
The U.K. benefited from some of that lovely oil wealth.
【Focus 1】全訳参照
Teaching English has morphed from being a mutually beneficial practice to becoming a massive international business.
英語を教えるということは互恵性のある実践から巨大な国際産業へと変化してしまったのです。

arbitrary
This system equates intelligence with a knowledge of English, which is quite arbitrary.
【Focus 2】全訳参照

Chapter 5
I. Understanding the Contents
問 1　b.　　問 2　b.　　問 3　d.　　問 4　a.　　問 5　d.

II. The Opinions
Focus 1
英語力ばかりが重視されるのは、教育が経済格差を生むからにほかならない。高収入の仕事は西欧の大学の出身者に与えられ、そのために親たちは子どもを西欧の大学に入れたがり、そのために英語力が重視されてしまうのである。

【全訳】
そう言えば最近こんな見出しを見ました。「教育——この大いなる格差」。もちろん、なぜみんなが英語にばかり目を向けるか、それはよくわかっています。子どもたちによりよい人生を与えたいからですよね。そのためには、西欧の教育が必要だというわけです。なぜかと言えば、いちばんいい仕事は、前にお話ししたように、西欧の大学を卒業した人間にいってしまうからです。堂々巡りのようなお話ですね。

Focus 2
ひとつの国の言葉しか用いないと、そこには思考の限界が生じる。別の言語を用いれば、その限界を超えた思考が可能になる場合がある。複数の言語が協力し合えば、私たちにとって新たな可能性がひらける。

【全訳】
さて、ここで2人の科学者、2人のイギリス人の科学者のことをお話ししましょう。2人は、動物の前肢と後肢に関する遺伝学的な実験をやっていました。しかし、思うような実験結果が得られませんでした。途方に暮れている2人の前に、ドイツ人の科学者が現れました。そのドイツ人の科学者は、イギリス人の科学者たちが前肢と後肢という2つの単語を使っているところに問題があるということに気がつきました。遺伝学的には前肢と後肢の区別はなかったんです。ドイツ語にも前肢と後肢の区別はありませんでした。お見事！これで難題が解けました。あることを考えることができなければ、私たちは行き詰まってしまいます。しかし別の言語を使えばそれを考えることが

できるわけです。協力しあえば、はるかに多くのことを成し遂げたり学んだりすることができます。

Focus 3

多様性が新たな発想を生む。世界中のいろいろな言語を大切にし、そしてそれを通じて、多様な発想を発信していくことが大切だ。

【全訳】

文字通りの意味での灯りであっても、比喩的な意味での灯りであっても、灯りを持たない人は試験にパスすることができません。そして私たちは灯りを持たない人の持っている知識を知ることができなくなってしまいます。灯りを持たない人たちを、そして私たち自身を、闇の中に置き去りにするのをやめましょう。多様性を称賛しようではありませんか。私たちそれぞれの言葉を大切にしましょう。それを用いて多様なアイデアを広めましょう。

III. Today's Vocabulary

prohibitive ← prohibit

They are prohibitive to so many millions of poor people.

それらは何百万人もの貧しい人々にとってはとんでもない出費になります。

differentiate ← difference

They were using two words for forelimb and hind limb, whereas genetics does not differentiate and neither does German.

【Focus 2】 全訳参照

credit

When students come to us from abroad, we may not be giving them enough credit for what they know.

海外から生徒が来るときに、私たちはその生徒たちが持っている知識に対して十分な承認を与えていない可能性があるということです。

consequence

A simple idea, but it could have such far-reaching consequences.

単純な考えですが、それは非常に大きな波及効果を持つ可能性があります。

celebrate

Let us celebrate diversity.

【Focus 3】全訳参照

Chapter 6

I. Understanding the Contents

問1　d.　　問2　b.　　問3　d.　　問4　c.　　問5　a.

II. The Opinions

Focus 1

現在の日本社会にとって最大の問題は、少子高齢化である。それが日本社会にもたらしたさまざまな問題を克服していくためには、日本を外に開かれたグローバル社会にしていくことが、ぜひとも必要である。

【全訳】

コロナ・ウィルス問題とかいろいろなことがあって、世界は大きく変化しつつあります。なによりも日本は高齢化社会——世界一高齢な社会です。だから若年層の人口減少はまず大学に影響を与え、それから社会全体に影響を与えます。病院や医師や社会保障手当を必要とする高齢者が増えて、その一方で働き手の人口が減少し高齢化していきます。だからそういう意味で日本社

会にかかるプレッシャーは日々増しています。それゆえに、日本のみなさんにとって、若い人々のためにより広い世界の一員となることが、大切だと私は思います。つまり海外に行って学んだり、日本で働こうという外国人を快く受け入れることができるようになることが大切です。

Focus 2

15歳のときには思いもかけなかったようなかたちで、自分はさまざまな国に旅し、住み、いろいろな言語を学んだ。その経験を通じて、視野が広がりそして人生が豊かになった。そのような体験は多くの人にとって大切である。

【全訳】

もし私が15歳のときに、「ルイス、おまえはいつの日か日本に住むことになるのだよ。お前は日本の大学に勤めて、日本で家を持ち、結婚して一児をもうけるのだよ」などと言われたら……そんなことが私の身に実際に起こるんだなどと言われたら、私は大笑いしてやったと思いますよ。正気ではないと思ったでしょう。そして若い頃の私を今から振り返ると、まあ悪い奴ではなかったとは思いますが、しかし視野の狭い人間でしたね。私の世界はほんとに小さかった。世界を旅したりいろいろな人に出会ったりして、私の世界は広がりました。そういう体験のおかげで、私にとっての世界はより広くよりよくなって、私の人生は15歳か16歳のときには想像もできなかったようなものになりました。だから複数の異なる言語を学び、旅をして、いろいろな場所に住むということは、かけがえのない経験です。素晴らしい。みんなそういう体験をすべきです。

Focus 3

言語と文化は切り離すことができない。それにあたる言葉がなければできない思考というものがある。だからある国の文化を理解するためには、その国の言葉をある程度まで学ぶ必要があるだろう。

【全訳】

それにあたる言葉がないような色彩を形容することは、私たちにはできない わけです。名前のない色彩は、イメージすることすらできません。私たちは 身についた言語によって制約を受けるんです。いつも必ず。日本語の中には あって英語の中にはない言葉があります。それは日本には存在して西欧には ない概念があるからです。そしてその逆のことも言えるわけです。つまり言 語と文化とは、驚くほど密接に結びついているということになります。日本 語を理解しなければ日本を理解することはできない。同様に、ある程度まで 英語を話すことができなければ、イギリスやアメリカやオーストラリアを理 解することはできないでしょう。

III. Today's Vocabulary

apply

After my PhD we applied for funding.

博士課程が終わってから、研究費を申請しました。

I nearly didn't apply.

もう少しで応募しないところでした。

initially ← initial

I came back to Japan initially as an English teacher.

私は当初英語の教員として日本に戻って来ました。

devastate

I was devastated because I was certain I wasn't going to get the job.

私は大ショックを受けました。なぜなら、絶対に面接に受からないだろうと 思っていたからです。

implication

When you've got a shrinking population of young people, then that has implications for universities first of all.

【Focus 1】全訳参照

invaluable

Learning different languages, traveling, living different places, is invaluable.

【Focus 2】全訳参照

Chapter 7

I. Understanding the Contents

問1　d.　　問2　b.　　問3　c.　　問4　c.　　問5　a.

II. The Opinions

Focus 1

「言語が私たちの思考を形作っているのか？」という当然の疑問について、古代から延々と終わりのない議論が繰り返されてきた。しかしごく最近になって、科学的なデータを用いて、この疑問に答えることができるようになった。

【全訳】

言うまでもありませんが、この世界にある言語はひとつだけではありません。7000ほどの異なる言語があります。そして、どの言語も他の言語とは、いろいろな意味で異なります。異なる音素があったり、異なるヴォキャブラリーがあったり、それから違う構造があったりします。とくにこの構造の違いが重要です。そこで当然浮かぶ疑問は、「言語が私たちの思考を形作っているのか？」というものです。これは古代からある疑問です。これについて、終わりのない議論が交わされてきました。神聖ローマ帝国のカール大帝は、「2

つ目の言語を話すことは、2つ目の魂を持つことである」という言葉を残しています。これは言語が現実を構築するということを強く述べた言葉ですね。しかしそのいっぽうで、シェイクスピアはジュリエットに「名前などどうでもよいのでは？薔薇になんという名前をつけても、同じように芳しいのです」という台詞を語らせています。これは言葉が現実をつくることなんてないということのようですね。こういう、ああでもなくまたこうでもないという議論が何千年も続いてきたわけです。ただこの議論に決着をつけるためのデータというものが、ごく最近までありませんでした。最近、私の研究所やそのほかの研究所で研究が始まり、この疑問に新たな光を当てるような科学的データを私たちは手に入れるようになったのです。

Focus 2

「左」「右」にあたる言葉をもたないクウク・サアヨッレの人々にとって、時間は常に東から西に流れる。つまり時間の流れは空間の中で定められている。それに対して西欧人にとっては、時間の流れは体の向きによって定まるものである。

【全訳】

では、先ほどお話ししたクウク・サアヨッレと呼ばれるアボリジニーの人々はどうするでしょう？彼らは「左」と「右」にあたる言葉は使いません。ヒントをあげましょうか。南向きに人を座らせたときには、クウク・サアヨッレの人たちの時系列は左から右になります。北に向いたときには、右から左になります。東を向いているときには、手前に向かって時間が流れます。どういうパターンかおわかりですね。東から西ですよね。だからクウク・サアヨッレの人々にとっては、時間は体につくのではなく、風景につくわけです。一方私にとっては、私がこちらの方向を向いていれば、時間はこの方向に流れ、それとは違うあちらの方向を向けば、時間はあちらの方向に流れます。私が体の向きを変えるたびに時間の方向がそれにくっついてくるなんて、いかにも自己中心的です

よね。クウク・サアヨッレの人たちにとって時間は風景の中で固定されています。これは時間というものに対する非常に異なる考え方です。

III. Today's Vocabulary
transmit

We can transmit really complicated thoughts to one another.
私たちは非常に複雑な考えをお互いに伝達することができます。
Because of this ability, we humans are able to transmit our ideas across vast reaches of space and time.
だから、この能力のおかげで、私たち人間は膨大な時空間を越えて自分たちの考えを伝えることができるのです。
We're able to transmit knowledge across minds.
私たちは知識を頭から頭へと伝えられます。

speculate

People have been speculating about this question forever.
【Focus 1】全訳参照

suggest

That suggests that maybe language doesn't craft reality.
【Focus 1】全訳参照

across

Because of this ability, we humans are able to transmit our ideas across vast reaches of space and time.
〈transmit の項を参照〉
We're able to transmit knowledge across minds.

〈transmit の項を参照〉

This is a big difference in cognitive ability across languages.

これは言語による認知的能力の大きな差です。

distinguished ← distinguish

Where one group—very distinguished group like you guys—doesn't know which way is which, but in another group, I could ask a five-year-old and they would know.

片方の集団—皆さんのように非常に際立った方々—は、何がどの方向かまったくわからないのに対し、別の集団では5歳の子どもに聞いてもわかるというわけです。

apply → appliance

You learn how to apply it.

あなたはそれをどのように当てはめるかを学びます。

Chapter 8

I. Understanding the Contents

問1　b.　　問2　b.　　問3　b.　　問4　d.　　問5　c.

II. The Opinions

Focus 1

地球上の言語の数が減っていくということは、数多くの異なる世界観を生み出すことのできた人間の知性の柔軟さを見失わせる。そしてアメリカの英語を話す大学生だけを被験者とした研究は、人間の知性についての私たちの知識を偏ったものにしている。

【全訳】

言語学的な多様性の素晴らしいところは、人間の知性がいかに精緻でまたいかに柔軟であるかを明らかにしてくれるという点にあります。人間の知性は、たったひとつの宇宙の認識を生み出すだけではなく、それを 7000 も生み出したのです。つまりこの世界では 7000 の言語が話されているのです。そして私たちはさらに多くの言語を作り出すことだってできます。言語というのは言うまでもなく生き物です。私たちが必要に応じて磨いたり変えたりすることのできるものです。ところが悲しむべきことに、私たちは言語学的な多様性を絶え間なく失いつつあります。私たちは 1 週間に 1 言語を失っており、地球上の言語の半分がこれからの 100 年間のあいだに失われてしまうという試算もあります。さらに悪いニュースがあります。それは私たちが人間の知性と人間の頭脳について知っていることのほとんどすべては、アメリカの大学の英語を話す学部生について行われた調査に基づいているという点です。それはほとんど全人類を除外するに等しいですよね。そうでしょう？だから私たちが人間の知性について知っていることは実際には信じ難いほどに狭くまた偏向したものだと言えます。現代の科学は、もっとまともなことができるはずです。

Focus 2

言葉が変われば思考も変わるということを述べてきたが、これは異国の人たちの思考という問題ではない。これは私たち自身がなぜこのような考え方をするのかを問い直すきっかけであり、それが新たな思考を生む。

【全訳】

お別れの前に、最後にお話ししておきたいことがあります。異なる言語を話す人々が異なるものの考え方をするということをお話ししてきたわけですが、これはもちろんどこかよその国の人の考え方という問題ではないんです。これはみなさん自身が、どのようなものの考え方をするかという問題です。

あなたの話す言語が、どのようにあなた自身の思考を形作っているのかという問題です。そうであれば、みなさんはこのように自問することができるでしょう。「なぜ私はこういうふうにものを考えるのだろう？」「どうすれば違うものの考え方ができるだろう？」そして「私たちはどのような新しい思考を生み出したいのだろう？」と。

III. Today's Vocabulary
distinguish
Russians have this lifetime of experience of, in language, distinguishing these two colors.
ロシア人たちは言語でこれらの2つの色を区別する経験を一生積んで来ているのです。

discriminate
When we test people's ability to perceptually discriminate these colors, what we find is that Russian speakers are faster across this linguistic boundary.
人々がこれらの色を知覚的に識別する能力を測ると、ロシア語話者たちはこの言語的境界を越えた2色の違いを識別する方が速いということがわかるのです。

consequence
Could this actually have any consequence for how people think?
このことは実際問題として人々がどのように考えるかということに何らかの影響をもたらすでしょうか？
Now, this has consequences.
さて、このことは重大な帰結をもたらします。

implication ← imply

This has implications, of course, for eyewitness testimony.

もちろん、このことは、目撃証言に密接に関わります。

It also has implications for blame and punishment.

またこれは非難や懲罰にも関わります。

as opposed to

I say, "He broke the vase," as opposed to, I say, "The vase broke."

私は「花瓶が割れた」と言うのとは対照的に、「彼が花瓶を割った」と言います。

You will blame someone more if I just said, "He broke it," as opposed to, "It broke."

私が単に「それが壊れた」と言うのではなく「彼がそれを壊した」と言っただけで、より誰か人を非難するようになるのです。

variety

I've given you a few examples of how language can profoundly shape the way we think, and it does so in a variety of ways.

言語が私たちの考え方を作り上げていることについて、どんなに深いレベルでそれが行われているかについていくつか例を挙げて来ましたが、実際それはさまざまな形で行われています。

Chapter 9
I. Understanding the Contents

問1　a.　　問2　b.　　問3　b.　　問4　c.　　問5　d.

II. The Opinions

Focus 1

使う言語を切り替えると性格が一変するとは思わないが、しかしどういう言葉を使うグループの中にいるかによって、振るまい方や言葉の使い方が変わるということはあるように思える。

【全訳】

K: 使う言語を切り替えると、性格とか自己表現まで変わるんでしょうか?

X: そうですねえ。性格まで変わるとは言えないんじゃないでしょうか。私の場合、どんな言語を使っていても私はいつも私です。いつでもそうですけど、私はおとなしい方で、ちょっと恥ずかしがり屋です。グループの中にいるとき、私はよく発言する方ではありません。だから性格までは変わらないと思います。でもどの言語を使うかによって、私の振る舞い方が少し変わるかもしれませんね。

K: 何か例を挙げていただけますか?

X: 例えばたくさんの日本人がいてミーティングに参加していて、そこである
トピックについて討議されているとすると、私はあまり活発に発言しない
かもしれません。私は意見を求められない限り、自分からは発言しない
でしょう。 たぶん私は静かにしています。そう期待されているからです。
でも中国人のグループの中にいるときには、私は好きなように行動し、ど
んどん発言します。英語を話す人たちのグループの中にいる場合も、たぶ
ん同じでしょう。

Focus 2

英語を学ぶために大切なことは、まず恥ずかしさを克服してともかく使ってみること、可能ならネイティヴ・スピーカーがいる環境に留学すること、それが無理ならネットを活用してできるだけ英語に接すること。

【全訳】

X: 言葉の学習についての日本のみなさんへのアドヴァイスですか……。言葉を学ぶのであれば、実際に使って練習しなければなりませんよね。まず何よりも恥ずかしさを克服しなければなりません。完璧に使いこなそうなどと思わないことです。ともかく学んだ表現を使って話してみましょう。たとえ正しく使えなくても、それでもまず使ってみましょう。だんだん使いこなせるようになるはずです。そう、それがまず第一ですね。もし私が日本人の親で、自分の子どもに英語を学ばせたいとしたら、そうですね、たぶん、機会があって、財源があれば、その子をネイティヴ・スピーカーがいる環境に送り出す（留学させる）と思います。昔は、私たちの身のまわりに英語を話す人がいなくて、テープレコーダーで、英語を聞いていましたもの。

K: そうでしたよね。覚えてます。

X: ビデオも映画もなかったでしょ。今では（聞きたいものは）なんでも手に入りますから。

K: そうですよね。オンラインで聞くことも、身の回りの人たちからも聞くことができますから。

Focus 3

せっかく日本に来ても、日本語を学ぼうとしない研究者がいるのは残念なことだ。言語を学ぶことは、その国の文化を知り人を知ることであり、そしてそれにより友だちができるというのは、素晴らしいことだ。

【全訳】

X: 日本に来る外国の人たちの中には、研究にしか興味を持たないという人もいます。そういう人は日本人と話す機会を避けてしまったりしますね。研究所によっては、例えば中国人がいっぱいいて、（そこでは）日本人だって英語を話します。だから英語ばかり使うようになります。あるいは日本

語を使ったり、日本語を学んだりせずに、母国語を使ってしまったりします。それはとても残念なことですね。そういう環境の中にいれば、わざわざ外国に行かなくても、外国語を学べるんです。せっかくそういう環境にいるんですから、それを活かして外国語を学ぶべきじゃないですか。

K: それに言葉だけではなく、その国の文化も人も学べるわけですね。

X: そう。友だちを作ることです。私は基本的にそうやって日本語を学んだことになります。

K: そうですね。友だちを作れるっていうことが、いちばんありがたいことではないでしょうか。言葉を知れば知るほど、その国の人たちのことを学ぶことができますよね。

X: いろいろな異なる言語を学んで、異なる文化に生まれた人たちを理解できるようになるって、素晴らしいことだと思います。

K: 人生が豊かになりますよね。

X: ずっと楽しくなりますよ。

III. Today's Vocabulary
serve
We can only serve research institutes that have contract with us.
私たちは契約関係にある研究所に対してしか支援を行うことができません。

institute
We can only serve research institutes that have contract with us.
〈serve の項を参照〉
Some people of course get hired by the Japanese research institutes.
一部の人たちはもちろん日本の研究所に就職します。

resource

If I have the financial resources, I will send that kid to a native-speaking environment.

【Focus 2】 全訳参照

pity

I think it's such a pity.

【Focus 3】 全訳参照

gift

The greatest gift is that we can make friends.

【Focus 3】 全訳参照

Chapter 10

I. Understanding the Contents

問1 d.   問2 b.   問3 b.   問4 d.   問5 a.

II. The Opinions

Focus 1

シングリッシュのような英語のバリエーションが存在することは、英語が劣化したことを意味するわけではない。英語がグローバルに使用されれば、多様な目的に合わせて英語が変化していくのは避け難いことである。

【全訳】

会議のあと、私はたまたま会議中にオフィスの前を通りかかった同僚にばったりと出会った。彼女は、部屋の中から怒鳴り声が聞こえてきたので、いったい何事かと思ったのだそうだ。私が以下の3点を説明しようとしたとき、

お役人のひとりが激怒してしまったのだと私は彼女に説明した。(1) シングリッシュが存在することと、英語の水準がどのようなかたちであれ低下したこととのあいだには、必ずしも相関関係は存在せず、まして両者の因果関係を示す証拠はまったくない。(2) 英語の水準が実際に低下しているということを客観的に確かめることは不可能とは言わないまでも極めて困難である。なぜなら言語の新しい使い方と誤った使い方とを厳密に区別することなどできないからだ。そして (3) 英語がグローバルに広がったということは、英語がさまざまな社会に定着するとともに変化していくものだということ、そしてさまざまな使用者がいろいろなコミュニケーションを目的として英語を受容するのみならず応用するものだということを認めなければならない。

Focus 2

激しい意見の対立にもかかわらず、私は「正しい英語運動」に招かれこれを受けた。政府は反対派の取り込みを狙ったのであろうが、私はシングリッシュと標準英語とのあいだの関わりについて誤解を解く機会として活用することにした。

【全訳】

この激しい議論にもかかわらず、政府は私を「正しい英語推進運動」に招聘した。辛辣な解釈(そして必ずしも的外れではない解釈)をするなら、政府は「トラブル・メーカー」になりかねない人物を仲間に入れて取り込んでしまおうとしたのだということになるだろう。それにもかかわらず、私はこの招聘を受けることにした。言語に関わる問題、そしてとりわけシングリッシュと標準英語をめぐるさまざまな誤解について政府の代表者と徹底的に話し合うよい機会になると考えたからだ。

III. Today's Vocabulary
adopt

There will be changes to the language as it takes root in different societies and is both adopted and adapted by various users for multiple communicative purposes.

【Focus 1】全訳参照

adapt

There will be changes to the language as it takes root in different societies and is both adopted and adapted by various users for multiple communicative purposes.

【Focus 1】全訳参照

tolerate

The indignant civil servant accused me of being far too willing to tolerate variations in language use.

その憤慨した官僚は私が言語使用のさまざまな形態に関して寛容であろうとしすぎると言って私を責めた。

provide

I thought it would provide me with a good opportunity to engage in extended discussions.

【Focus 2】全訳参照

engage

I thought it would provide me with a good opportunity to engage in extended discussions.

【Focus 2】全訳参照

assumption ← assume

I thought it would provide me with a good opportunity to engage in extended discussions with government representatives about language matters and, specifically, about various assumptions concerning Singlish and Standard English.

【Focus 2】全訳参照

Chapter 11

I. Understanding the Contents

問1　b.　　問2　c.　　問3　a.　　問4　d.

問5　And because the issue involving the Singlish controversy are by no means unique to Singlish but are in fact relevant to broader concerns about language and identity in the context of globalization, I am hopeful that the discussion in this book will be of interest to a fairly wide audience and not just those concerned with promoting or retarding the use of Singlish.

II. The Opinions

Focus 1

シングリッシュについての論争は硬直し、議論をすればするほどシングリッシュの擁護派と反対派とのあいだの亀裂はいっそう深まり、お互いの立場を理解し合うというような好ましい結果に結びつくことはなかった。

【全訳】

公の場でシングリッシュのことが議論されるたびに、同じ議論が持ち出され、そして同じようなレスポンスが示されるという傾向がみられる。その結果としてすでに確立されてしまった考え方や態度（思い切り単純化してしまえば、シングリッシュは「良い」ものか「悪い」ものか、それゆえにシングリッ

シュの擁護派か反対派かという二分論）がいっそう頑強になった。心と心が近づいたり、異なる立場がよりよく理解できたり、議論の背後にあるイデオロギー的な前提についてより柔軟な理解ができるようになったりということが、まったくなかった。

Focus 2

シングリッシュをめぐる私の立場は現在でも変わっておらず、シングリッシュ反対派に対して私は批判的である。しかし擁護派の意見も反対派の意見も、それぞれに問題をはらんでおり、それぞれの前提を見直す必要がある。

【全訳】

しかし、ここではっきりと述べておきたいのは、何年も前に私がなんとかしてあの政府高官に伝えようとした論点は、いまでも有効だということである。それゆえに私は、シングリッシュが問題であるとか、取り除かれるべき言語学的な害悪であるとかいった考え方に対して、概ね批判的である。しかし、だからといって、シングリッシュ擁護の立場で提起された議論に問題がなかったということではない。シングリッシュの擁護派の打ち出した議論も、反対派が打ち出した議論も、等しくあやふやな前提に基づいているという傾向がある。

III. Today's Vocabulary

appreciation, appreciative ← appreciate

I came to be more appreciative of the kinds of pressures that civil servants work under.

私は官僚たちがどのような圧力の下で働いているかについて、より理解できるようになった。

Running an official campaign such as the Speak Good English Movement meant being answerable to politicians and members of the public about how resources were being spent and having to show that some 'progress' was being made each year (such as reducing the rampant use of Singlish, raising awareness of the importance of Standard English or simply increasing appreciation and sympathy for the Movement's goals).

「正しい英語を話す運動」(Speak Good English Movement) のような公的な活動を行うということは、政治家や一般の人たちに対して、資源がどのように使われているかについて答えられることを意味するし、毎年多少の「進歩」があること（例えば盛んにシングリッシュが使われるのを押さえ込むとか、標準英語の重要性に対して注意を喚起するとか、単にこの運動の目的に対する理解や共感を増すだけでも）を示す必要があるということを意味するのだった。

There is no evidence of a closer meeting of minds, a better appreciation of different positions or a more nuanced understanding of the ideological assumptions involved.

【Focus 1】全訳参照

premise

There has been no significant change in the premises and parameters of the debate.

この論争における前提や条件に関する大きな変更はないままだった。

point

The points I tried to convey to that senior civil servant all those years ago remain valid.

【Focus 2】全訳参照

liability

Viewing Singlish as a liability or an asset in fact sidesteps many of the important and complicated issues involved.

シングリッシュを欠点か利点かと捉える見方は、実際のところ、この問題に
関わる多くの重要かつ複雑な論点を回避してしまうことになる。

asset

Viewing Singlish as a liability or an asset in fact sidesteps many of the
important and complicated issues involved.

〈liability の項目を参照〉

Chapter 12

I. Understanding the Contents

問 1　c.　　問 2　d.　　問 3　c.　　問 4　c.　　問 5　b.

II. The Opinions

Focus 1

タガログ語がフィリピンの国語のベースではあるが、しかしフィリピンには
非常に多くの方言があり、タガログ語を特権化することへの強い抵抗がある。
それゆえに英語やスペイン語と混淆したフィリピン語が国語となっている。

【全訳】

H: 歴史的に言えば、私たちにはタガログ語があります。でもフィリピンには
　たくさんの地域的な方言があります。そしてタガログ語はフィリピン北部
　の方言ですから、他の地方の人々はフィリピンがタガログ語を国語の基盤
　としたのは不公平だと感じるわけです。ですから厳密に言えば、フィリピ
　ンの国語はフィリピン語ということになります。でもフィリピン語はタガ
　ログ語が基盤になっています。そしてタガログ語は方言のひとつなのです。

K: そうなんですか。知りませんでした。ということは、フィリピン語とタガログ語はイコールではないということですね。

H: そうです。ですからフィリピン語と言った場合、それはタガログ語にスペイン語が混じり、英語が混じったものです。混成言語ですね。クレオール語のようなものと言っていいでしょう。このあたりの細かい事情を知っているフィリピン人は少ないんです。だから「フィリピンの国語はなんですか？」と聞かれたら、私は必ず「フィリピン語です」と答えます。憲法にきちんとそう書かれているからです。

K: 「フィリピンの言葉は何？」って聞かれたら、私などは「タガログ語です」と答えてしまいそうですけれど、それは間違いなんですね。

H: ええ、違います。フィリピン語なんです。

K: 初めて知りました！

H: 「F」で始まるフィリピン語（Filipino）ですよ。かつては「P」で始まる綴りだったんですけど、綴りが変更されたんです。

K: どうして？

H: フィリピンという国の歴史的な背景を顕彰するためです。私たちにはスペイン語がありアメリカ英語があり、さらにローカルな言語があります。フィリピンが混淆した文化であるということを強調するためですね。それでも、やはり国語のベースがタガログ語であるのは公平ではない、セブアノ語やヒリガイノン語もあるのに、と言う人たちもいるんです。公平さに欠けるとそういう人たちは考えます。フィリピンに行けば、タガログ語を絶対に話さないという人がいることに気がつくでしょう。そういう人はタガログ語を受けつけないんです。

Focus 2

生まれた時から英語に接しているという意味では、自分はネイティヴ・スピーカーである。しかし「ネイティヴ・スピーカー」というイメージは、国籍・

出身地に強く結びついてしまっているから、自分はネイティヴ・スピーカーとはみなされてはいない。

【全訳】

K: ご自分は英語のネイティヴ・スピーカーだというふうに考えますか？

H: バイリンガルの英語ネイティヴ・スピーカーだと考えています。ネイティヴ・スピーカーの定義の仕方っておもしろいなと思います。いろんなネイティヴ・スピーカーがいて、いろんなアクセントで英語を話すんです。多くのフィリピン人は、生まれたときから英語を学び、身につけ、英語を聞いて育つんです。でも必ずしも英語を話すとは限りません。それは英語で人に話しかけると気取っているととられるからです。「なんで訛りのないきれいな英語なんか話すの？」みたいな。英語は唯一の言葉であってはいけないんです。少なくとも2つの言葉を話すことになっているわけです。

K: 自分がネイティヴ・スピーカーだとみなされていると感じますか？

H: いいえ。そうは思いません。ネイティヴ・スピーカーというものをどう定義するか、どう見るか——そこにはヒエラルキーのようなものがあると思います。ネイティヴ・スピーカーを出身地や国籍で定義しているんじゃないでしょうか。もっぱらパスポートの問題ですね。だからネイティヴ・スピーカーって、本当はきちんと定義されていないようにも思えます。私はインドやパキスタン出身で、きちんとした英語を話す人をたくさん知っています。そういう人たちも、自分はネイティヴ・スピーカーだと感じているでしょう。ただ私もそういう人たちもそれぞれ違うアクセントで話します。そうなったのは私たちのせいではないと思いますよ。グローバリゼーションのせいですよね。英語がこんなに世界中に広がるのが嫌なら、アメリカ人やイギリス人は海を渡ったりせず、私たちを放っておいてくれればよかったですよね。しかし放っておいてはくれなかった。だからいろいろな種類の英語が話されるようになったんです。

Focus 3

日本では、「ネイティヴ・スピーカー」というと、青い目で金髪の白人というイメージに結びついている。これは単純なイメージの問題ではなく、経済と深く結びついている。

【全訳】

とくに日本では、ネイティヴ・スピーカーというとき、まず外見から判断されているように思えます。青い目で金髪の典型的な白人であるかどうか。どこの国の出身か。アメリカ、カナダ、イギリス、オーストラリアの出身かどうかとか、延々と続きます。そしてフィリピンはそういう格付けのいちばん下にくるわけです。そういう見方になるのには理由があります。それは日本人が抱くネイティヴ・スピーカーのイメージだけの問題ではありません。経済だと思います。

III. Today's Vocabulary

concern

My research concerns art.

私の研究は美術・芸術に関係しています。

discourage

And so it was to discourage you from using your national language.

そしてつまりあなたが国語を使うことをやめさせようとしたわけですね。

technically

So technically speaking, the national language is Filipino.

【Focus 1】全訳参照

accept
They don't accept it.
【Focus 1】 全訳参照

perceive
Do you feel that you are perceived as a native English speaker?
【Focus 2】 全訳参照

fault
And you can't fault us, because of globalization.
【Focus 2】 全訳参照

Chapter 13

I. Understanding the Contents
問1　b.　　問2　b.　　問3　c.　　問4　b.　　問5　d.

II. The Opinions
Focus 1
ひとつのグローバル言語を定めれば、みんなが同じ土俵に立つことができるとも言えるが、しかしそれは西欧中心主義に結びつく危険もある。

【全訳】
K: そうなると、ひとつのグローバルな言語を共有したほうがいいという議論にもなりますね。ひとつの言語を共有していれば、みんな同じ土俵に立つことになるんじゃないでしょうか？

H: そうですね。でもグローバル言語としての英語、という考え方には問題があります。それは植民地主義にもつながります。

K: それはほんとうに問題ですね。その通りです。

H: ヘゲモニーです。西欧文化のヘゲモニーです。

Focus 2

英語を世界共通言語とすることは、自分のような英語既習者にとってはありがたいことであり、また英語は比較的習得しやすい言語である。しかし、それは西欧中心主義にも結びつくという問題がある。

【全訳】

K: 英語を世界共通言語にすべきだと思いますか？なぜそうか、あるいはなぜそうではないかお話しください。

H: これは単純には答えることのできないご質問ですね。私はすでに英語を話しますから、英語をグローバルな言語とすることは、私にとっては有利です。新しい言語を学ぶことがどのくらい難しいかよくわかっています。これだけ長いあいだ日本語を勉強して日本に住んで、それでも日本語は私にとって習得するのが難しい言語です。たとえ日本人であっても、一生かかって習得するくらい難しい言語ですよね。私はよく学生たちに、英語のアルファベットには26の文字しかないんだよなんて言います。辞書をひくのも簡単です。たった26文字ですから。でもこの問題をさらに深く考えれば、それは植民地化の歴史の問題ですよね。西欧文化のヘゲモニーです。しかしその一方で、今、歴史のこの段階まできて、選択の余地があるのでしょうか？　英語ですか？　それとも中国語ですか？　数字の上では中国語を話す人の方が多いわけですから。

Focus 3

エスペラント語のような人工的に作られた言語を共通語にすればよいという考え方もある。しかし膨大な学術的文書がすでにインターネット上にある現状では、それを放棄したりすべてエスペラント語に翻訳したりするのは現実的ではない。

【全訳】

K: エスペラント語を共通語にすべきだ、エスペラント語という人工的に作られて固有の文化に結びつかない言語にすべきだとも考えてきました。

H: でもその場合、過去になされたすべての研究とすべての文書を、つまりすべての文書とすべての学術的な知見を、ご破産にすることになりますよね。すべてをエスペラント語に翻訳するんですか？

K: 鋭いご質問ですね。インターネットのおかげで選択の余地がなくなってしまいましたね。いまやすべてがインターネットにあげられて、すべての人がインターネットに接続しているわけですから。英語が事実上の共通言語になってしまったと言ってもいいでしょうね。

III. Today's Vocabulary

integrate

The better you are at speaking Japanese, in a way you get more integrated into the culture.

日本語がうまくなればなるほど、ある意味ではその文化に統合されていきます。

invest

We've stayed here and tried to invest in learning.

私たちはここに滞在して、［日本語を］学ぶことに打ち込んできたんです。

You're investing in trying to learn.

あなたは学ぼうとすることに注力しています。

I am invested in this country.

私はこの国に価値を見出しているんです。

case

Maybe it builds a case for having a global language.

【Focus 1】全訳参照

issue

At the same time, there are issues around it, English as a global language.

【Focus 1】全訳参照

If you go deeper into the issues, this is the history of colonization.

【Focus 2】全訳参照

assimilate

People treat you better if they think you are stupid than if you try to assimilate.

あなたが同化しようとするより、みんながあなたのことをバカだと思えた方が、みんなあなたに親切にするんです。

Chapter 14

I. Understanding the Contents

問1　d.　　問2　a.　　問3　c.　　問4　c.　　問5　a.

II. The Opinions

Focus 1

グローバル市民とは、国籍・民族・信仰といったアイデンティティーを放棄することなく、しかしグローバル社会の一員でもあるという自覚と責任感を持ち、その行動を通じてグローバルな価値観に寄与しようとする人間である。

【全訳】

私は、自分をグローバル市民だと考えています。つまりいまあらわれつつあるより大きな社会の中に自分を見出し、そして自分の行動を通じてそのような社会の価値観に寄与するような人間です。そうであっても、私は自分の国である

南スーダンへの忠誠といったアイデンティティーを放棄するつもりはありま
せんし、自分の民族性や信仰を放棄するわけでもありません。そういった伝統
的なアイデンティティーは、私の人生に意味を与え、そして私という人間を形
作ってくれました。それにもかかわらず、グローバル化する世界の中で生きて
きた結果として、私は新たなレベルでの責任というものをになうようになった
と思います。私たちは、同じひとつのグローバルなアイデンティティーを持っ
た世界規模のコミュニティーの一員としての責任をになっています。

Focus 2
地球規模のさまざまな問題を解決して、よりよい世界を未来に残していくた
めには、私たちがグローバル市民として、ささやかな行動を通じてささやか
に世界を変えていくことこそが大切である。

【全訳】
グローバルな経済の冷え込みを心配する必要のないような世界を想像してみ
てください。貧困との戦いが存在しないような世界を想像してみてください。
さまざまな問題について行動するほうが、行動しないことよりはるかに安く
つきます。もし私たちが行動するグローバル市民として、グローバルな問題
を解決する方法を探究すれば、そうすれば私たちはもっと平等で持続可能な
社会に生きることができるでしょう。行動は言葉よりも雄弁なのです。です
から、みなさんはぜひ立派なグローバル市民になっていただきたいと思いま
す。いまある問題を解決しなければ、私たちの地球を救わなければ、私たち
の言葉が無意味であれば、いったいどのような未来を私たちは作るのでしょ
う？ケニアの女性環境保護運動家であるワンガリ・マータイさんの言葉を借
りるなら、市民がするささやかな行動、それが世の中を変えるのです。この
世界をごくささやかにでも変えることを通じて、後世に記憶されたいと思い
ませんか？

316 | English for Global Communication

III. Today's Vocabulary

recognize

What is the correct concept in which this responsibility is recognized?

この責任をきちんと扱える正当な概念とはどのようなものでしょうか。

Global citizenship is defined as a way of living that recognizes that our world is increasing web of connections and interdependencies.

グローバル・シティズンシップとは、私たちの世界がますます密接に関連し、相互依存の網目の中にあるということを認識するような生活の仕方であると定義されます。

due

It is due to our selfish reasons that food production is affected and as we speak, Kenya faces food shortages due to recurring droughts.

私たちの我儘な理屈のせいで食物生産が影響を受けており、ちょうど今この瞬間も、ケニヤは度重なる干ばつが原因で食糧不足に直面しています。

This is due to preventable causes like poverty and malnutrition.

これは貧困や栄養失調など、避けることができる原因によって引き起こされています。

embrace

I appeal to all of you sitting here to embrace the idea of a global identity.

私はここに座っているみなさんに、グローバル・アイデンティティーという概念を受け入れていただけるよう訴えます。

belonging, obligate → obligation, oblige

I believe that global citizenship is the key to shaping our future because it helps us create a sense of belonging to a common humanity, creating a fairer world and hence helping learners to feel obligated and responsible to be active global citizens.

私はグローバル・シティズンシップが私たちの未来を創る鍵だと信じています。なぜなら、それは私たちに共通である人類に属しているという感覚を与え、より公平な世界を創り、そのことによって学習者が積極的なグローバル市民となる義務や責任があると感じるようになることを助けると考えるからです。

civic, involve

This is a form of civic learning that involves students' active participation in projects that are just global issues of an environmental, political, social, or economic nature.

これは市民としての学習のひとつの形態であり、環境的、政治的、社会的、または経済的な性質を持つグローバルな問題を扱うプロジェクトに、生徒たちが積極的に参加することを伴います。

Chapter 15

I. Understanding the Contents

問1　b.　　問2　b.　　問3　c.　　問4　b.　　問5　b.

II. The Opinions

Focus 1

つくばインターナショナルスクールは、人類の多様性を尊重し、グローバル市民としての意識を涵養する「国際的思考」を目指している。それに従い、英語のみによる教育ではなく、言語の多様性を尊重した教育を行っている。

【全訳】

ですから私たちの「国際的思考」の自前の定義は以下のようなものです。こ

れは生徒から保護者から教員から役員までみんな含んだコミュニティーの中
での共同的な模索の結果として生み出されたものです。私たちはみんなで集
まって「国際的思考」のさまざまな側面について考え抜きました。そして以
下の5点にまで煮詰めることができました。つくばインターナショナルスクー
ルでは、「国際的思考」をこのように定義します。

- ・人類の多様性を理解し、受け入れ、賞賛する。
- ・自らのアイデンティティーを意識するとともに、文化・信教・価値観
  の異なる他者を尊重する。
- ・グローバルなコミュニティーに参画し、多様なものの考え方を身につ
  けるとともに、同じ人間であるという信念、地球という同じ惑星を守っ
  ていくという信念を涵養する。
- ・自分の言葉で語り、他人の言葉にオープンに耳を傾けることにより、
  他人の身になり共感を持ってコミュニケートする能力。
- ・世界をすべての人にとってよりよい場所とするために貢献し行動する、
  責任あるグローバル市民であること。

だから以前は、インターナショナルスクールの教室では、「英語だけ。英語だ
けしか話してはいけません。日本語が聞こえたら承知しませんよ」みたいな
言い方がされました。それは、必要もないのに盲腸を切除してしまうような
ものです。そんな必要はぜんぜんなくて、その言語は理解を助けるために役
立ちますし、英語がいちばん優れた言語であるわけでも唯一の言語であるわ
けでもないということに気づくためにも役に立ちます。世界中にはさまざま
な言語があって、英語はその中のひとつに過ぎないんです。生徒が家庭で話
すときに使う言語もかけがえのない価値を持ちます。それを使って別の言語
を学ぶことができ、その言語もまたもうひとつの道具にすぎません。英語は
利用することのできるもうひとつの道具だということです。ひとつの言語が
別の言語より優れているとかそういう考え方は必要ないんです。

Focus 2

英語が共通言語になったことは否定しがたい。それは歴史の偶然のもたらした結果である。将来に期待したいことは、シンガポール英語やクレオール語など世界各地の英語のバリエーションを同列に置いて見られるにようになることである。

【全訳】

英語が共通語であると思います。それは議論の余地がありません。あなたや私のようなカナダ人、とくに英語を話すカナダ人は、ラッキーだったということですね。勝ち組になってしまったわけです。英語を話す人間は、グローバル言語は何かというコンテストで当たりくじを引いたようなものです。私は英語がそれ自体としてよい言語であるとか偉大な言語であるとかは考えません。歴史的な偶然でそうなっただけです。歴史のある段階で大英帝国が世界中に拡張して掌握したり……。 その結果として、英語がこんなふうに世界中に広がったわけです。それでいいのか、英語が偉大な言語かどうか——それは私にははかり知ることができません。最良の言語とは思わないです。すごく複雑でいろいろな例外を含みますから。でもグローバル言語であるという現状は否定しようがありません。私が将来に期待したいことは、英語のさまざまなバリエーションが平等に受け入れられるようになることです。例えば、あなたと私はカナダ英語を話します。そしてアメリカ英語があり、イギリス英語があるわけです。でもそれはネイティヴ・スピーカーがいろいろな異なるアクセントで話しているというだけのことです。できることなら将来には、そういうさまざまな英語が、シンガポール英語とか日本英語とかインド英語とか、どこの国で話されるどのような英語とも同列であるとみんなが納得できるようになることを、私は期待します。そしてすべての人のための英語になること、ネイティヴ・スピーカーが話す多様な英語の多様なバリエーションですね。だから、例えばかつてはアフリカ系アメリカ人の英語は、英語の劣化したかたちととらえられる傾向がありました。中米やカリブ海のあ

る地域で話されるクレオール語もそうです。そういう言語は劣った英語とされてきたわけです。私はそういう英語が、劣った英語ではなく、同じくらい有効な英語の一形態として理解されるようになるとよいと思います。

III. Today's Vocabulary
assign
I was assigned to a really, really, tiny village in Fukushima prefecture.
私は福島県のすごくすごく小さな村を割り当てられました。

figure
I really couldn't figure out where I was going. So I just had to arrive in Japan and start looking at maps that were made in Japan to figure out where I was going to be in that prefecture.
私は自分がどこに行くのか本当にわかりませんでした。だから、とにかく日本に着いて、その県の中で自分がどこに居ることになるのかを割り出すために、日本で作られた地図を見始めました。

celebrate
Understanding, accepting, and celebrating human diversity.
【Focus 1】全訳参照

engage
Engaging with the global community to gain a variety of perspectives.
【Focus 1】全訳参照

argue
I think there's no arguing that we, as Canadians, as English-speaking

Canadians in particular, were just lucky.

【Focus 2】全訳参照

inherently ← inherent

I don't think that there's anything inherently good or great about English.

【Focus 2】全訳参照

著者紹介

宮本　陽一郎（みやもと・よういちろう）

1955 年	東京都に生まれる
1981 年	東京大学大学院人文科学研究科課程修士課程修了
1981 – 83年	東京大学助手
1983 – 94年	成蹊大学講師・助教授
1994 – 2017年	筑波大学准教授・教授
2018年〜	放送大学教授
現在	放送大学教授・筑波大学名誉教授
専攻	アメリカ文学，カルチュラル・スタディーズ
主な著書・訳書	『モダンの黄昏—帝国主義の改体とポストモダンの生成』研究社、2002 年
	『アトミック・メロドラマ—冷戦アメリカのドラマトゥルギー』彩流社、2016 年
	『知の版図—知識の枠組みと英米文学』（共編著）悠書館、2008 年
	Hemingway, Cuba, and the Cuban Works.（分担著）Kent State University Press, 2014.
	ジョン・ガードナー著『オクトーバー・ライト』集英社、1981 年
	チャールズ・ジョンソン著『中間航路』早川書房、1995 年

大橋　理枝 （おおはし・りえ）

1970 年	京都に生まれるが、7 か月後に東京に引っ越し、そこで育つ
2000 年	ミシガン州立大学コミュニケーション学科博士課程修了（Ph.D. in Communication）
2001 年	東京大学大学院総合文化研究科言語情報科学専攻博士課程単位取得満期退学、助教授として放送大学勤務
現在	放送大学教授
専攻	異文化間コミュニケーション

主な論文・著書　『音を追究する』（共著）放送大学教育振興会、2016 年
『色と形を探究する』（共著）放送大学教育振興会、2017 年
『コミュニケーション学入門』（共著）放送大学教育振興会、2019 年
『英語で「道」を語る』（共著）放送大学教育振興会、2021 年
『ビートルズ de 英文法』（共著）放送大学教育振興会、2021 年
『異文化との出会い』（共著）放送大学教育振興会、2022 年
「『教養学部』であるために─新型コロナウイルス関連 YouTube 動画作成、及び BS231 放送番組制作の実践報告を起点に─」『放送大学研究年報』第 38 号、191-199、2020 年

Kristie Collins （クリスティ・コリンズ）

1974 年　　ノヴァ・スコシア（カナダ）で生まれ、1 歳からプリンス・
　　　　　　エドワード島（カナダ）で育つ
2008 年　　バーミンガム大学大学院博士課程社会学専攻単位取得退学
2007 – 2017 年　　筑波大学講師・准教授
2017 年〜　麗澤大学大学准教授
現在　　　　麗澤大学大学准教授
専攻　　　　ジェンダー・スタディーズ，TESL
主な著書・訳書　*The Marginalized Majority*: *Media Representation
　　　　　　and Lived Experiences of Single Women. Peter Lang,
　　　　　　2013.
　　　　　　Readings on Diversity Issues: *From hate speech to
　　　　　　identity and privilege in Japan*.（分担著）Living Within
　　　　　　Diversity Press, 2016.
　　　　　　Intercultural Communication in Japan: *Theorizing
　　　　　　Homogenizing Discourse*.（分担著）Routledge, 2017.

MEMO

放送大学教材　1420143-1-2211（ラジオ）

グローバル時代の英語

発　行　2022 年 3 月 20 日　第 1 刷

著　者　宮本陽一郎・大橋理枝・クリスティ コリンズ

発行所　一般財団法人　放送大学教育振興会

　　　　〒 105-0001　東京都港区虎ノ門 1-14-1　郵政福祉琴平ビル

　　　　電話　03（3502）2750

Printed in Japan　ISBN978-4-595-32358-4　C1382